I0510935

Black and White Photography

The art of making great black and

White photos

purposes only and is universal as so.

TABLE OF CONTENTS

BLACK AND WHITE

A concept all photographers need to remember when we are using our camera.
"You don't take a photograph, you make it."
-Ansel Adams

Here is an outstanding example of the subtle shading that makes making black and white shots so powerful. This has just a touch of sepia to make it brown.

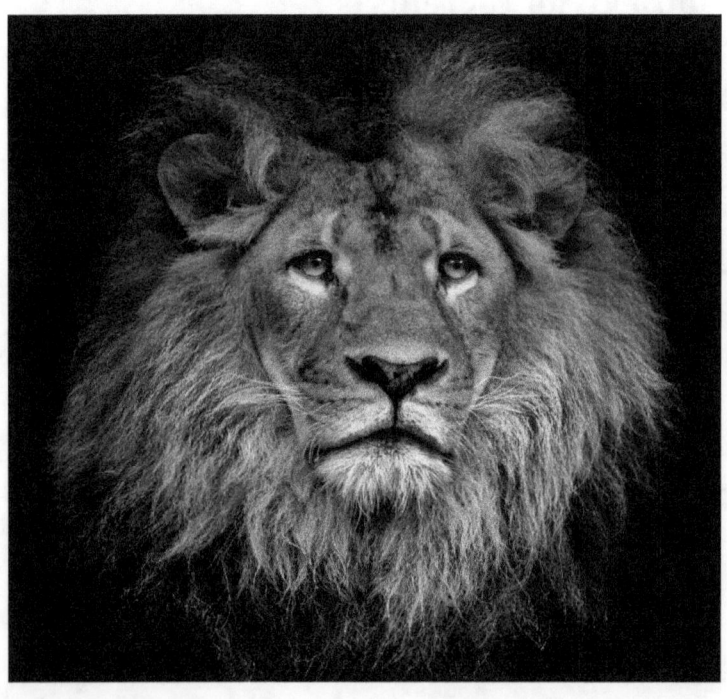

To take a photograph at its best, you need to explore the options to get the best look. I almost always make all shots in color. Then convert to black and white if the shot looks good in color. That way you always have a color copy. It is much harder to recolor a photo than take the color out if you ever want a color print of the shot.

I take shots in black and white, sometimes with my phone camera. Many times, it is beneficial to see the shot in black and white. It helps you learn to see shadows and tones in the shot different from what you see in color. It also makes texture pop out of the shot so you can see things you cannot see in color.

Most people like to see photos in color most of the time. It is the way most of us see everything. That is enjoyable, but it can take away from some important things we should see. There are situations where black and white is better. In high contrast photos black and white can be much more interesting. Making a shot black and white can also take an average photo and make it great.

Most viewers can also appreciate a great black and white shot, they look at it more like art than a photo. They also do not think it is a snapshot, it looks like you put time and thought into the shot. Here is a quick example of what I am talking about. The color shot is an ok shot, but the black and white shot has a different feel.

Notice the shadows and the texture in the wings. All I did was convert the shot to black and white in the app on my phone and the texture pops. The texture in the feathers is the first thing you see in the black and white, but not in the color shot.

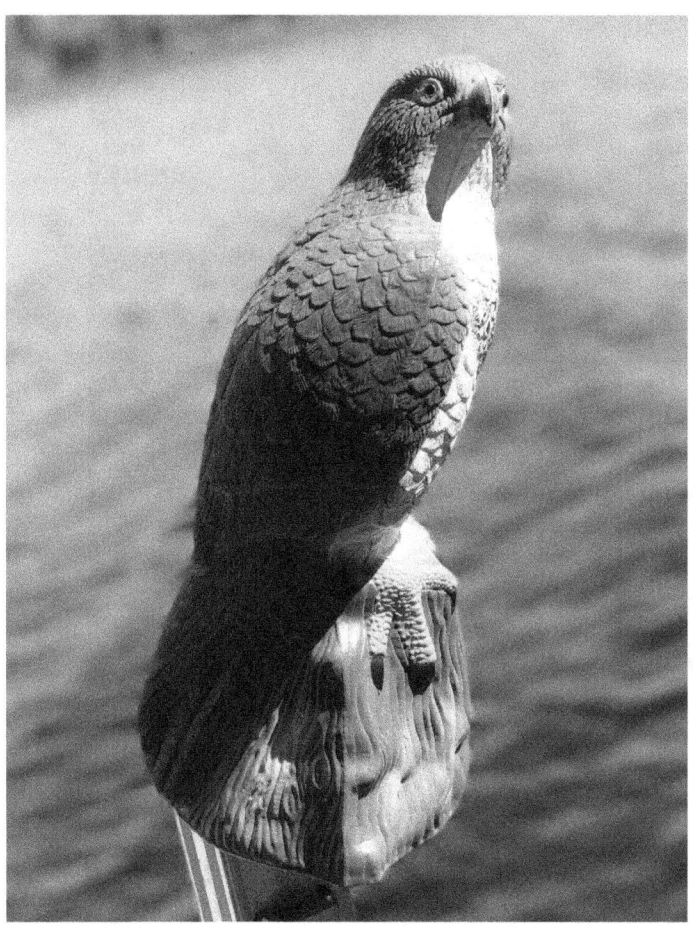

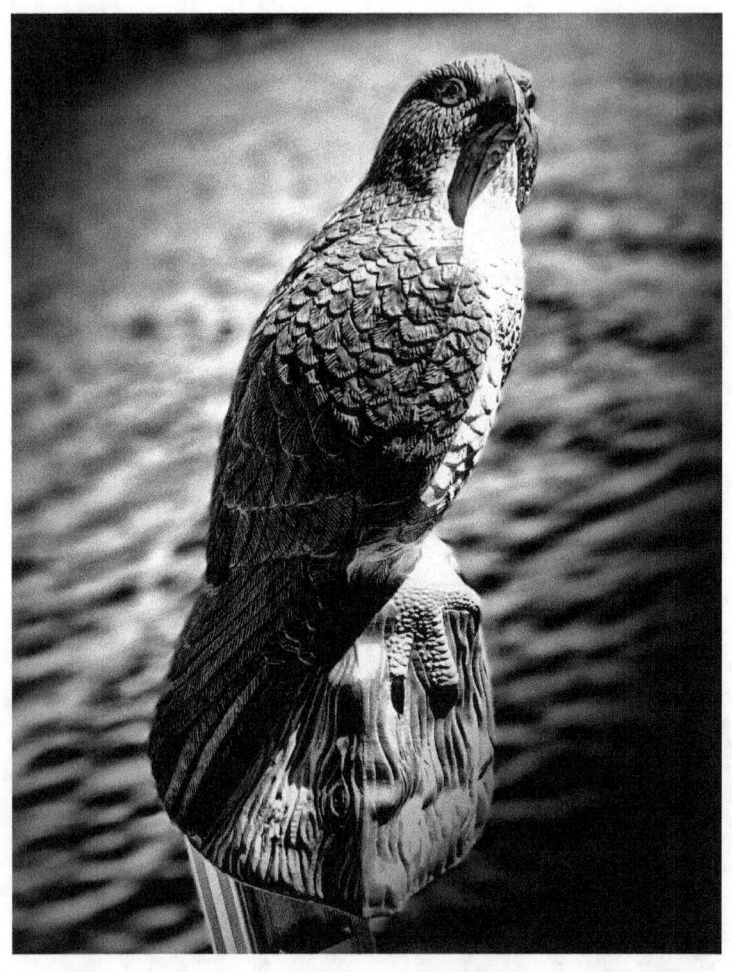

Black and white photographs are simplistic. Taking out the color changes the focus. The focus goes from the color to the composition and the creativity of the shot.

Color can distract from the shot. It can take the focus away from the subject, which is something you do not want to do. Look at the shot in color. What do you think it will look like without color? Do you think it may look better without color? Desaturate the shot and see what it looks like.

There are many ways to take out the color, but to look the best you need to do a few more things than desaturate only. We will get into that more later.

Why should you take photos in black and White?

- There can be many subtle tone differences you cannot get in a color photo.
- Black and white can bring out your creativity more than with color.
- You see light different in black and white than you do in color.
- Black and white brings out emotion in the shot.
- Black and white highlights form patterns and negative space.

- Without color, you see the interaction of the lines in the shot, to bring out the shapes and forms.
- Flat light shots also have more options to make a shot interesting. Most flat light shots are boring.
- Black and white photos can be much more dramatic.
- Bringing out texture is much easier in black and white photography.
- Learning to shoot well in black and white will make you a better photographer when shooting in color.
- Shooting black and white makes you focus more on the composition.
- Color will not distract from the creativity or the emotion of the shot.
- You can create a certain mood in the shot you cannot do in color.

In this book I will give you tips on how to take the best black and white shots you can. I will show you how to use black and white to change the mood of the shot and create the emotion you want to portray.

I have taken hundreds of thousands of photos over the past 40 years. Many have been black and white, or converted to black and white. I have studied photography in practice and at photography school many years ago. Practice is the best way to learn. Learn by using your eyes and other available tools to make the best shots you can.

Take time and search black and white photos online. Look at the variety of shots. Look to see what type of look you prefer. Do you like high key, dramatic, middle shades of gray, infrared, or do you like it with a tint to the shot?

Look at Ansel Adams photography. Look at other great black and white shots and see how the photographer sees the light. Look at how they compose the shot to create the shot they want.

If you have not tried black and white. Check it out and see what you can do. It is easy to make great shots if you learn what to look at.

Converting to Black and white

This is how you will create most of your black and white shots. Start with a color photo and create the black and white look you want. Black and white is still popular with many people. If you look at social media, you will see black and white is popular for viewers. If you are a serious photographer, and want to do more than take snapshots, you should look at black and white photography. You are stifling your creativity if you do not work with black and white.

The great thing about digital photography is that you have a world of options available in software. You can change and make a black and white shot look hugely different. You can make it more interesting to look at than bland color or desaturated monochrome photos.

Some types of photos lend themselves to black and white much better than other types of photos. Some types of photos must have color to be their best. Sunset shots would not portray the same mood or impact in black and white.

Old-fashioned and aged things make great photos in black and white. Black and white can change the mood and make the shot much more interesting. Old barns, farm machinery, broken down buildings all lend to great black and white photos. Close up faces of older people with lines and wrinkles make great black and white because of the texture it adds to the shot.

The first thing you should do is adjust the shot for the best color photo you can. In adjusting the color shot. Make the shot a little more saturated than you would in color. Also upping the contrast and even increasing the exposure will give you more leeway when converting. I also like to use a little tone mapping to increase the range of tone from black to white.

Once you get it adjusted for good color, then you can work on the black and white. When you start, always make a copy and work on the copy. Do not work on the original photo. That way you will not compromise the original. As you adjust the shot, if you get a cool look, save a copy. You can save copies at different places along the way for comparison. Many times, several of the saved copies will work well.

For some shots, one of these methods may give you the look you want. For many shots it will be a mixture of these methods to get the best look you can. Not one of these methods is better than another. They all give different results. Great black and white photos are a matter of personal taste for most. I lean toward a full tone coverage from black to as close to white as I can get, and higher contrast. Some people like varying subtle shades of gray. Using the full range makes the shot much more dramatic.

If you look at the shots from Ansel Adams. One of the best black and white photographers of all time. His shots were all dramatic and created a mood that would suck you into the shot. Look at his photos and see how he used light to the greatest extent he could to create the best dramatic moody shots he could. He did all this with his eyes and his camera. He spent hours, days and weeks setting up shots and getting it the way he wanted. We can do it so much easier now, but the techniques and concepts he used are the same now. His shots are all fantastic because he would not publish it until it was what he envisioned for the final shot.

The basic conversion method to get a black and white shot from a color shot is to desaturate the shot. This will take out all the color. It is a good first step sometimes. But it does not give a great finished shot for most situations. This method on its own sets all the tones to middle shades of gray. It is not too impressive by itself. If you desaturate and then do other adjusting, you can create a shot you will be proud of.

- After you adjust the color and desaturate the shot, open the brightness, then the contrast, and adjust it to a look you like. Most times I go minus on the brightness and up on the contrast. Play with it and see what you like.
- Once you get that set where you like the look, open the curves and play with the curves until you get what looks good.

Here is an example of what I did in a few minutes doing what is above. I took a good color shot and made it into a cool black and white shot.

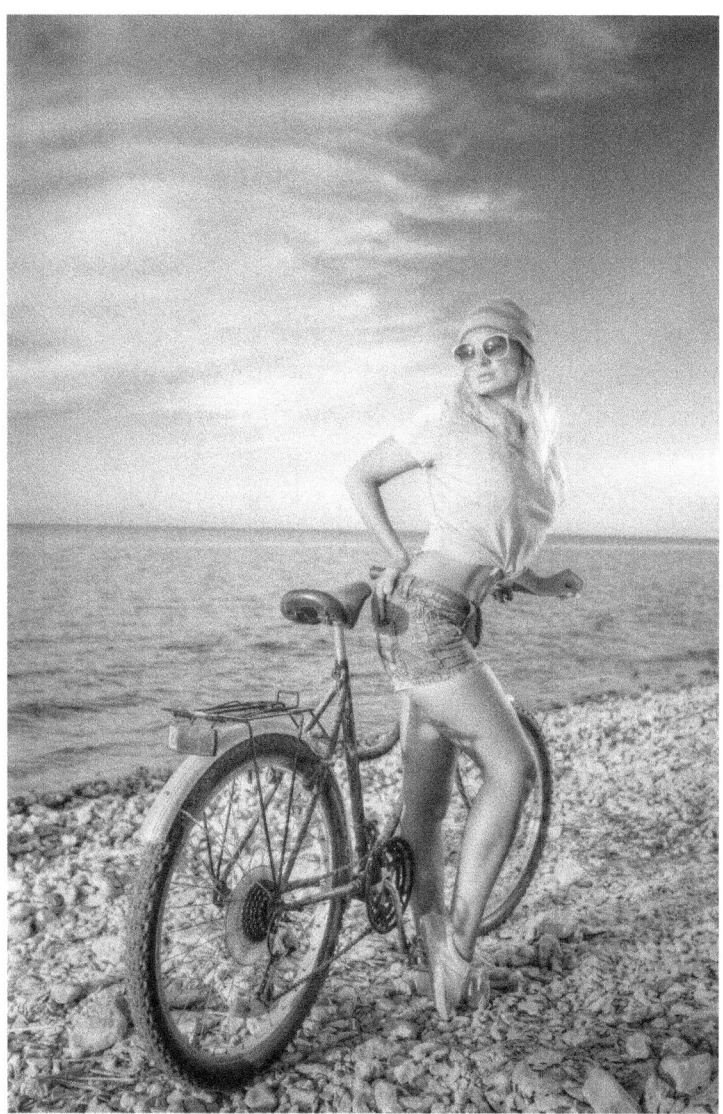

The color shot is a good shot. It is a cool looking scene, but it can be better with black and white. My goal with black and white or color shots is always making it look the best I can for the look I want. Ask yourself, when someone sees my shots, are they going to say wow, or cool or awesome? If not, try to make it better.

Notice how the light and shadows make the shot more interesting and better. Notice the tonal range, from black to almost white. Look how the darker sky is much more interesting and stands out so much more. The differences do not take away from the subject; they add to it. The subject is still the girl, but the shot is more interesting with the changes in the black and white.

The oldest and still a good way is to open the channel mixer. You can find this in most photo editing programs. Photoshop, Paint shop pro, gimp, and many other photo editing programs.

- Open the image and open the channel mixer. Select monochrome with the output channel to grey. Adjust the constant setting to where you think looks like a good place to start.
- Play with the different color channels and see what you like. Small adjustments make a big difference. Make small incremental changes to start so you can see what it

changes. There is a lot of math you can study to figure out the best way to set it. Going by look is the best method, that is what the viewer sees.

This shot I did a channel adjustment. Then did a little tone mapping and finished with a highlight mid-tone and shadow change to tweak it to the look I wanted. The black and white shot is much more dramatic. It would not work for certain applications, but it would for others.

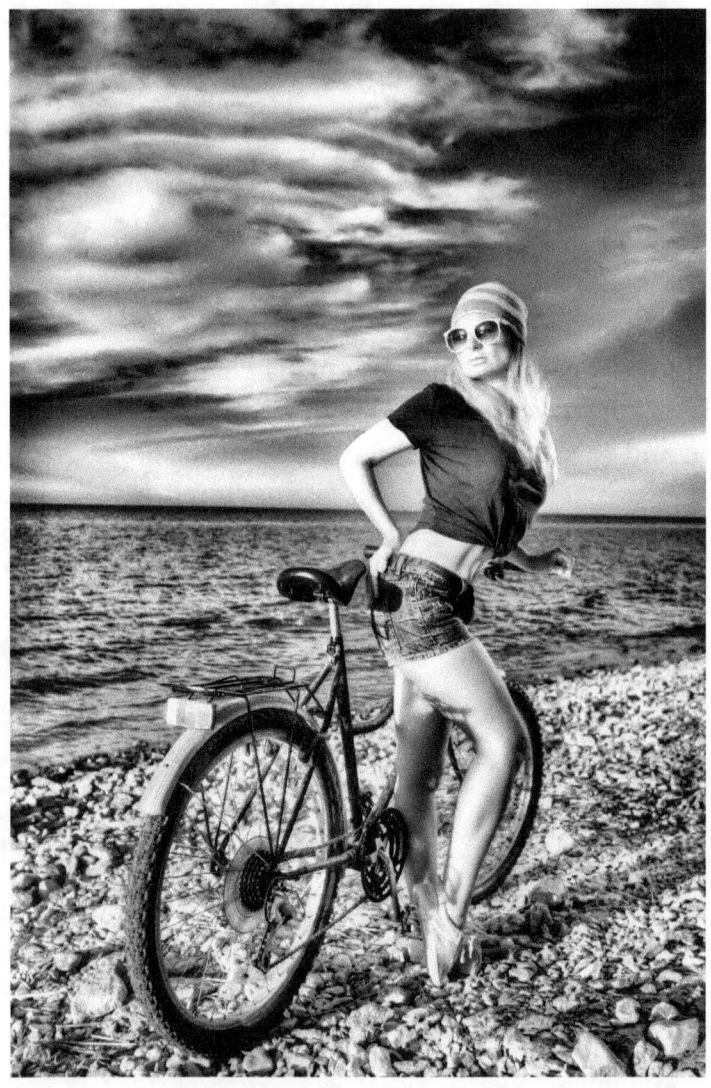

You do not even notice the sky in the color shot, but you do in the black and white, it is more dramatic, they both look good. It depends on what you are going for.

This one gave it a cool effect for a different look. Some people like this look. As you can see, there is no limit to what you can do with the same shot if you get creative.

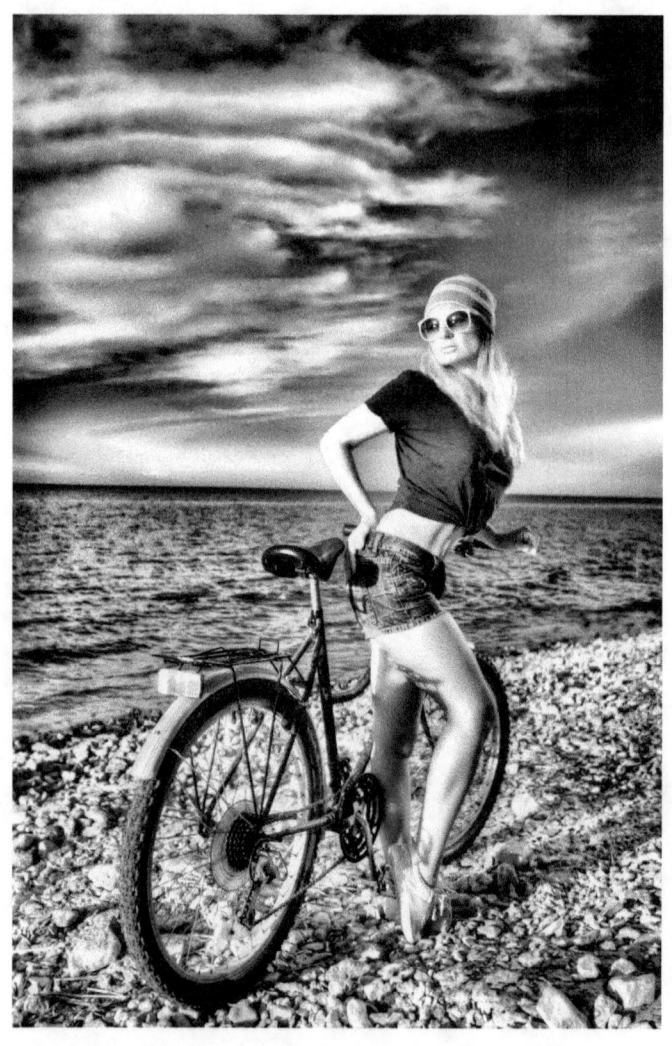

You can go on and on and get hundreds of different looks from the same shot. Knowing what you want the shot to look like when you start will give you an idea of how to go about it. There is not a right or wrong way to get the shot the way you want it. It is all about experimenting and trying the different methods until you get the shot you want.

Try using a curve change with the methods above. Like I said, there is not a right or wrong way to do this. You may like a different look than I do, but you can get there with these methods.

There are many other options you can use to get the look you want. You can get any look you want with these few simple tools. The key is to work on the shot to get the look you want to create.

GENERAL TIPS

"I am sure the next step will be the electronic image, and I hope I shall live to see it. I trust that the creative eye will continue to function, whatever technological innovations may develop."–Ansel Adams.

Ansel Adams saw the coming of digital photography. The freedom and flexibility available in digital photography should make the creativity really come out and we should be able to create stunning and meaningful photos.

- If you want to use the full range of creativity in your photos, shoot in raw. Shooting raw will allow you to cover the full spectrum of what is possible. Taking a photo that lives up to the image you see in your mind will happen much easier when you shoot in raw.
- When you are shooting knowing you want it to be black and white. Make sure you look at the shapes of the lines, the forms, and the shadows in the scene. Try to ignore the color.
- The best way to get the best black and white photos is to get the range of your shot to go from black to white. Covering the full range from true black to pure white will get you the

best shots. Using the levels adjustments in a photo editing program, try to get the full spectrum of tones from black to white. Try to adjust the levels from one end to the other.

- Be careful when sharpening black and white photos. It is easy to introduce noise into the dark parts of the shot when sharpening.
- One thing quite different about good black and white and great color shots is the time of day. Best color photo lighting is in early light, or late light. Black and white shots are many times best taken in the middle of the day when the sun is harsh. If you want to take photos in the middle of the day, look at black and white.
- If you want to take silhouettes, black and white is best for these shots.
- Many times, the best light for black and white is the most unflattering for shooting in color.

How to shoot in black and white

- Shoot in raw if you can.
- Shoot in color if you cannot shoot in raw.
- Shoot in black and white if you shoot in raw.
- Use the lowest ISO you can to avoid noise in the dark areas.

- Shoot black and white when you would not shoot in color. Shoot black and white on cloudy days and mid-day on bright sunny days.
- Compose your shots in black and white so you can see the shadows and lines.
- Use light and shadows in black and white.
- Focus on texture and shapes.

FILTER EFFECTS

Experiment with color filters and see what the best look of the tones are with the different filters. I have found that red filters give you the most contrast and the best look for landscape and outdoor shots. Yellow is a good choice for portrait shots.

Filter effect

Film photography filters can be added to the lens to alter the effects in black and white photography. Using colored filters would make the corresponding color of the filter lighter, and the opposite color darker. You can now apply these colored filters with software and get the effect without having to use physical filters on the lens.

How to use color filters.

These are the color filters used in black and white photography.

Red: Makes blue skies dark. Great for making shots more dramatic. If you tweak the contrast with a red filter, you can make the sky almost black. The contrast with a red filter is strong. Sometimes too strong for many types of photography.

Orange: Makes blue sky darker. Not as dark as red. Orange is between red and yellow. It gives a nice smooth skin look and works well on portraits.

Yellow: Will darken blue skies but is more useful for portraits. Yellow is subtle in the effect. Also works great for portraits that need some darkening and smoothing of skin tones.

Green: Will make greens lighter. Used to brighten and pop photos with lots of greens. Good for foliage in outdoor and landscape shots. Gives separation in shots with lots of foliage. Good for flower shots.

Blue: Blue filters get less usage. They darken most colors and even out the contrast. They can work well for some photos. Try them and see how they look.

Here is the same shot with color, desaturated and each filter.

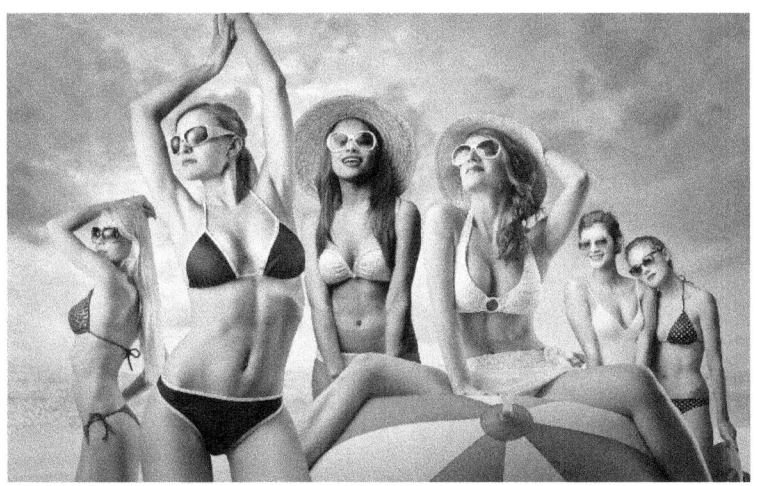

DESATURATED

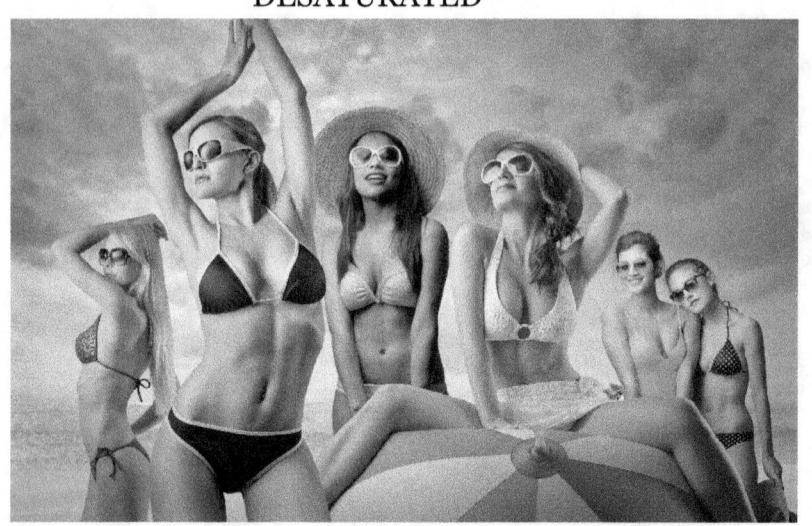

RED

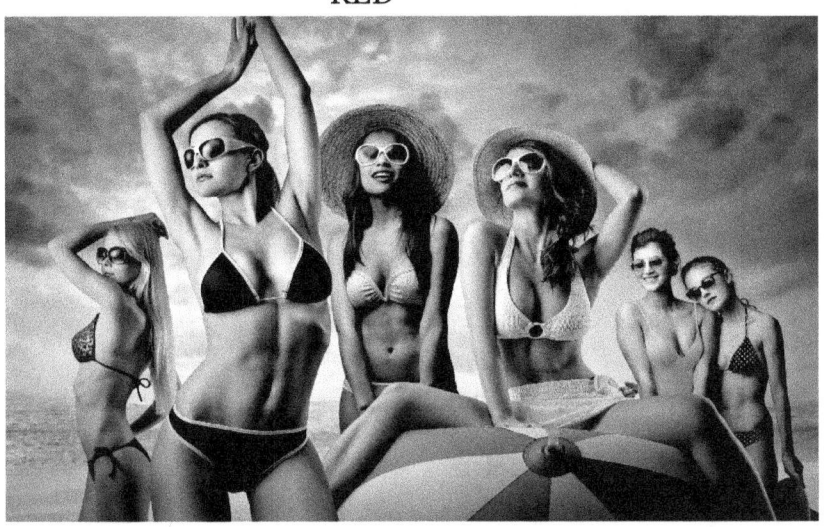

GREEN

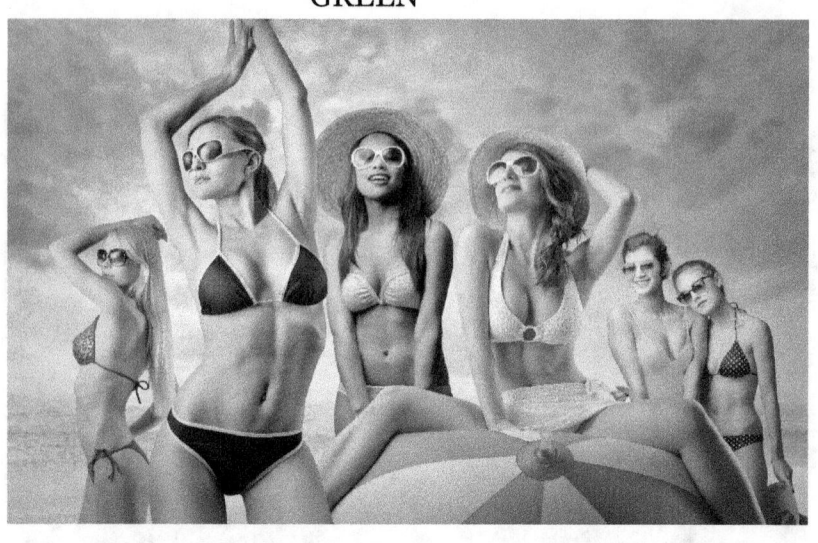

BLUE

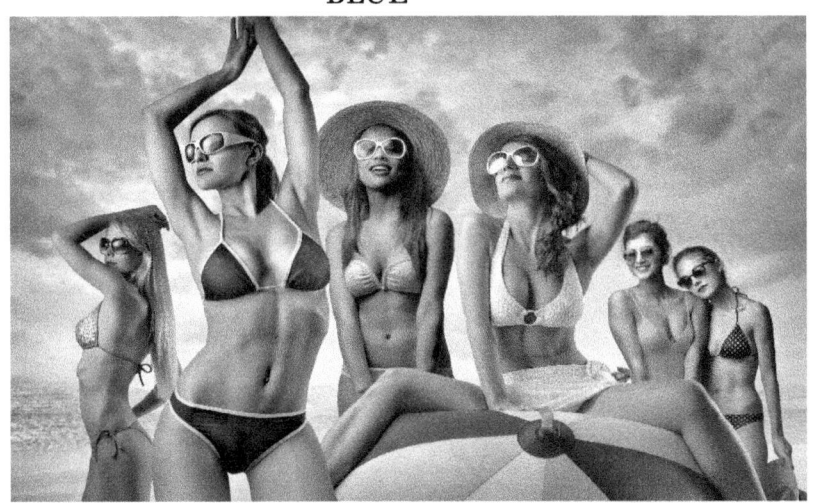

YELLOW

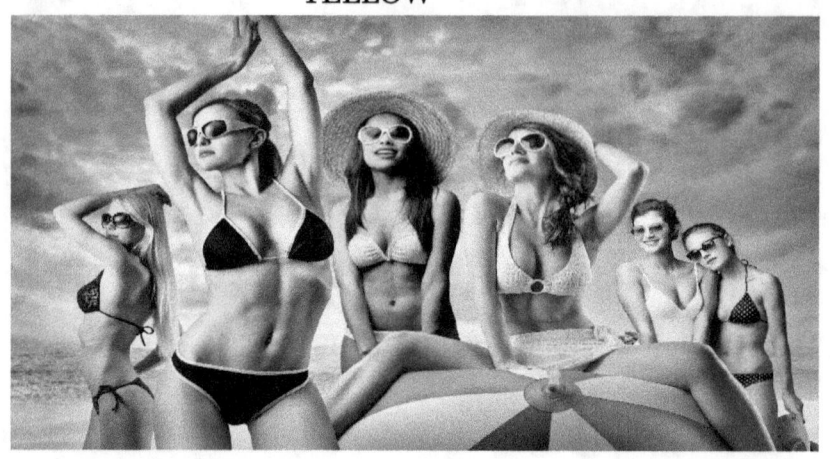

Orange

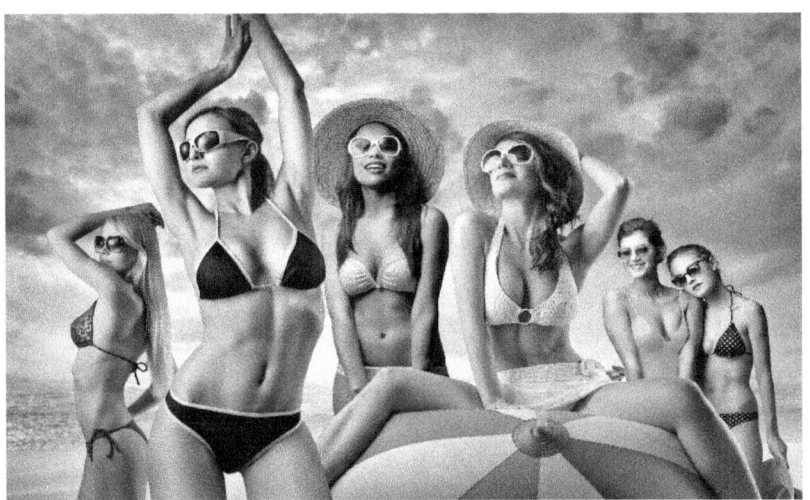

Some color filters do not change the shot much. Some do. The red filter is the most dramatic. Blue is next in contrast variation. The green is another one I use a lot. The shot above works in color or black and white depending on the look you are going for. Some differences are subtle. You can see it in the skin tones and the shadows on the skin. The sky changes a lot with the different filter choices.

LANDSCAPES

Landscapes and street photography lend themselves to great black and white photos. You can have more contrasting shots and shots where light and shadows can play a big role in how the shot looks. Decaying things, things that are rundown, and things in disrepair almost always can make great black and white shots.

- One key to great black and white landscapes is having a good contrasting sky, or at least a stormy sky. A bright blue sky with lots of big puffy clouds is the ideal sky for making great landscapes in black and white. If the sky is a big part of your shot, a blue sky with no clouds is not as good. For color shots, many times, bright blue sky is the best.
- Using HDR for making great black and white shots. HDR is a great tool for making dramatic black and white shots.

Here is a shot I took on the beach in St Pete's beach Florida a couple months ago. The shot is a nice shot of the beach. I used an HDR filter in a photo editing software and then desaturated it and came up with this.

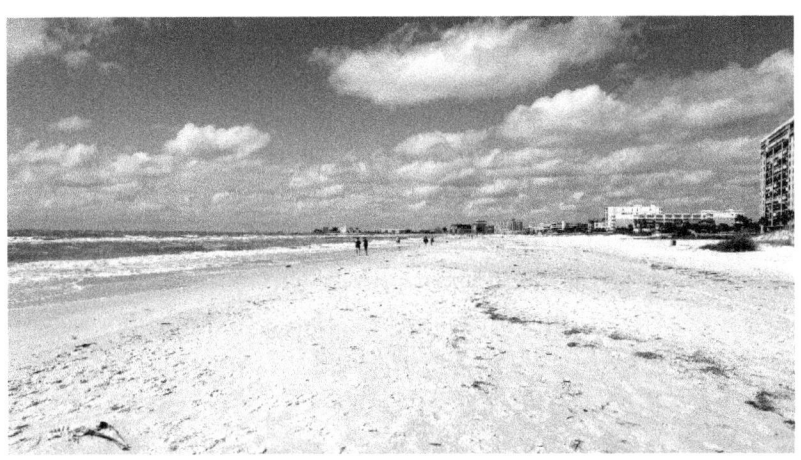

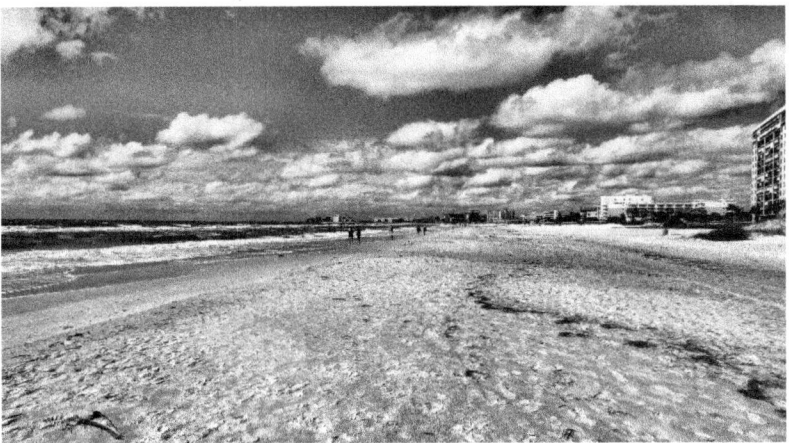

If you will use this method of converting, take the original and use the HDR filter. Do it at about 25%, save it. Then desaturate it and see how it looks. See if it is too much or too little. Go back and adjust the amount of HDR to get the look you think looks best.

Do not overdo it, even in black and white, you can overdo the HDR.

Use the clouds. Clouds add a lot to the drama of black and white shots. A blue sky with lots of puffy white clouds will give a better look and add drama to the photo. Look at the shot above, the clouds make a big difference in the shot. The clouds add to the color shot somewhat, but they add a lot to the black and white shot.

Look at the sand in the colored version and look at the sand in the black and white. See how the tones pop out. The tones are very subtle in the colored shot, much more dramatic in the black and white. This is what you are looking for when trying to make a dramatic black and white shot. Notice the footprints in the black and white. In the color shot you do not see them at all. In the black and white they are one of the first things your eyes get drawn to.

This shot I took off the dock. I thought the sky was interesting looking. In color, this shot was not impressive. In black and white It is kind of cool looking. The clouds are dramatic, and the tone goes from black to white and all the variations of gray between.

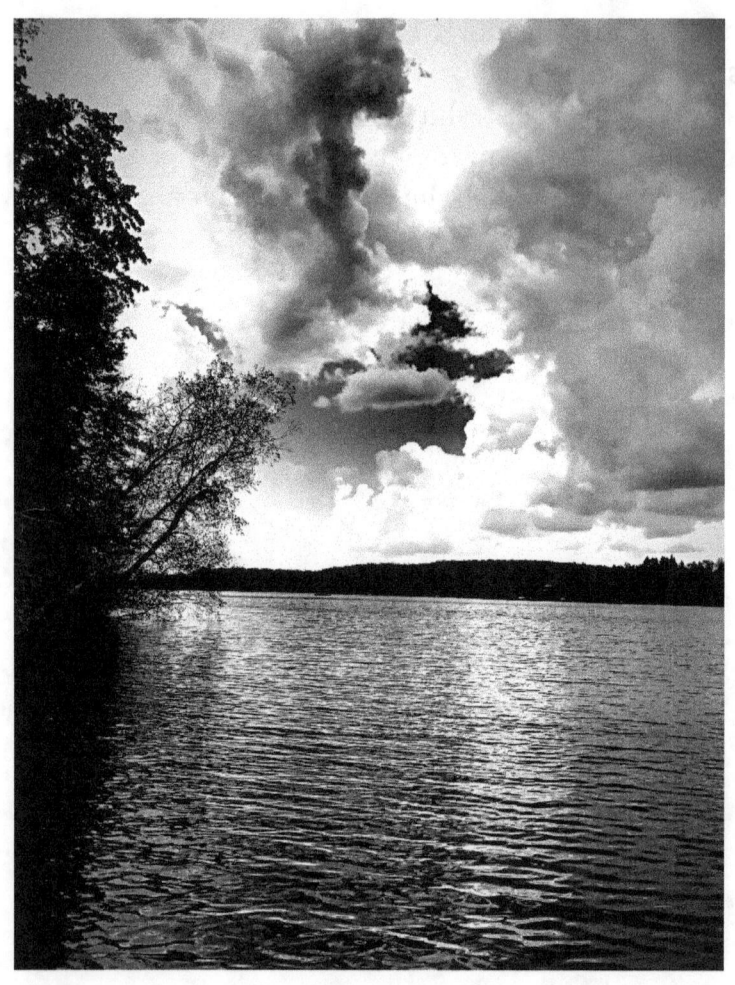

My wife and I were in New Orleans a few months
ago. This shot, taken by my son-in-law. It is a nice

shot, but the exposure was bad on the upper right side. Between the house and the tree, on the right, the sun was blowing out the highlights. I tweaked it and it would not look good in color. When I converted it to black and white, it made it a cool shot. The more I looked at it, the more I liked it.

It would be even better without the people in it. The point is I took a good subject and fixed a not so good photo to make it a usable photo that is interesting. This shot looks better being less dramatic. It helps pull out the details in the fence and the trees.

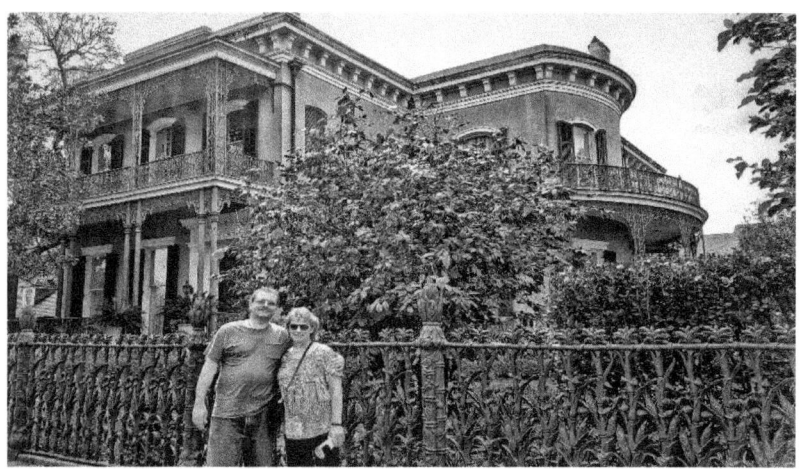

This shot in color was not interesting. It looked like a fire pit with stuff behind it. After converting to black and white, it becomes an interesting shot. The smoke from the grill is much more visible. The shading difference between the wood that has burned and the wood yet to burn has a cool look. The more dramatic background contrast also adds to the shot.

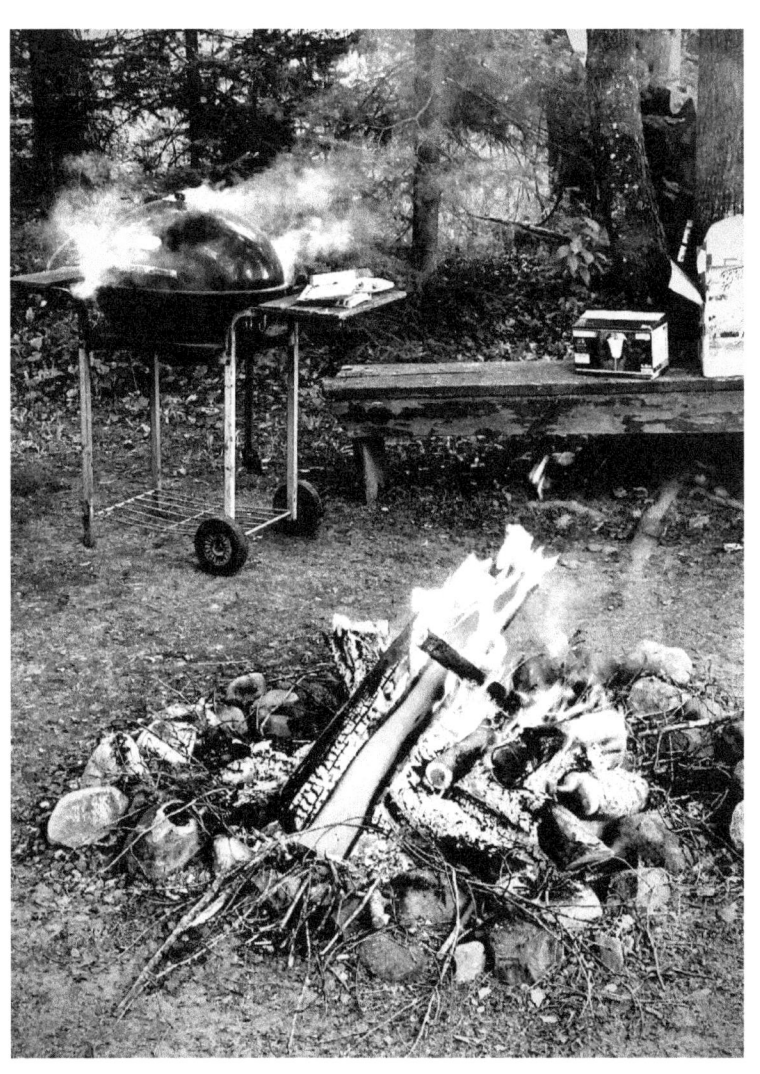

We have an old boathouse at the cabin that has been falling apart for years. The roof is no longer there, and the rocks are falling off the walls. It looks like a rock dugout on the side of the hill. In black and white the shot looks cool and interesting. There is a spring that comes out of the hill in the middle of the back wall. It runs all the time feeding the lake.

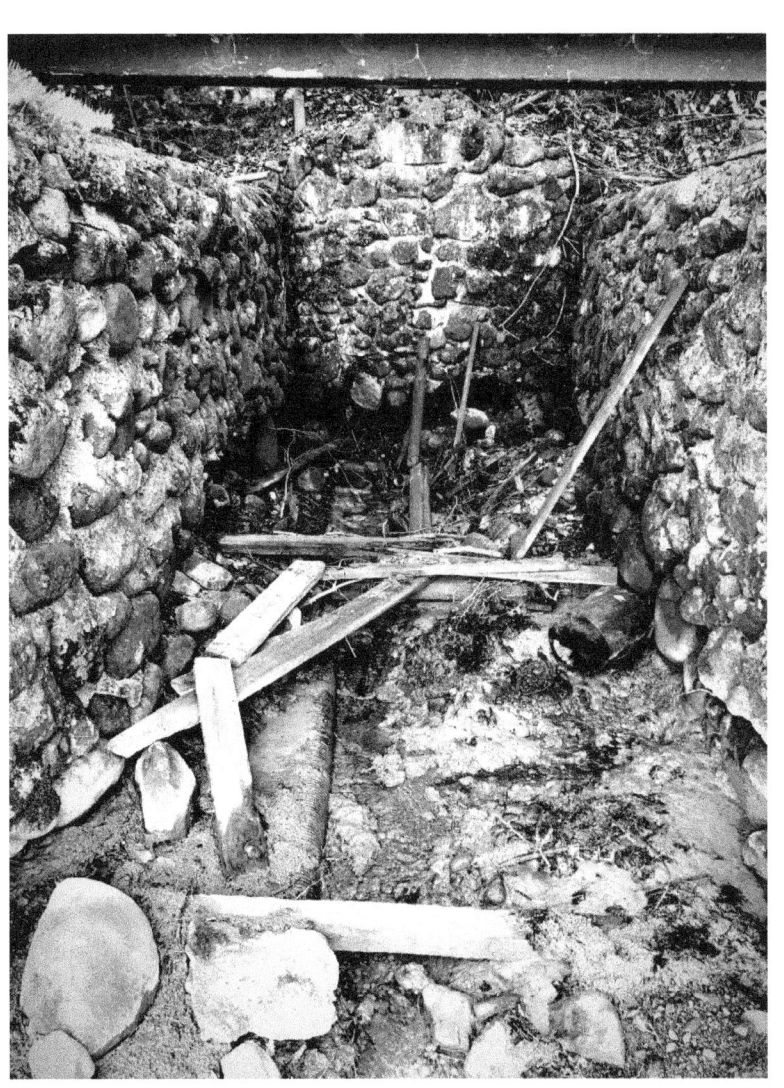

This shot I took standing in the door of my townhouse. Looking out toward the water tower. This shot is not anything anyone else would say is interesting. I converted it to black and white and used an infrared filter on it. Then I used an app on my phone called reflect to add the water in the foreground. There is no water anywhere around here. It is a fake shot, but it looks cool and interesting. It looks like I took the shot from a flooded-out parking lot or flooded stream.

See how I framed the water tower with the trees? It is the obvious subject of the shot, but all the other pieces of the photo work together and add to the shot.

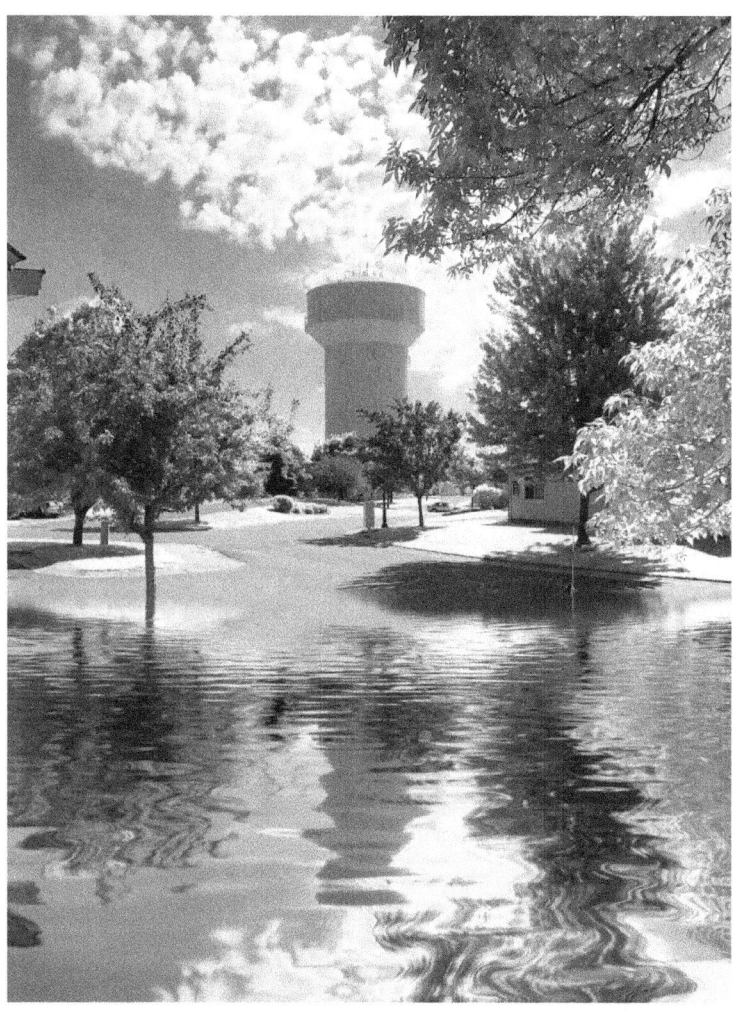

Here is a dramatic winter shot I took at a park not far from my house several years ago. Good clouds for contrast and the snow on the ground makes the shot look cool.

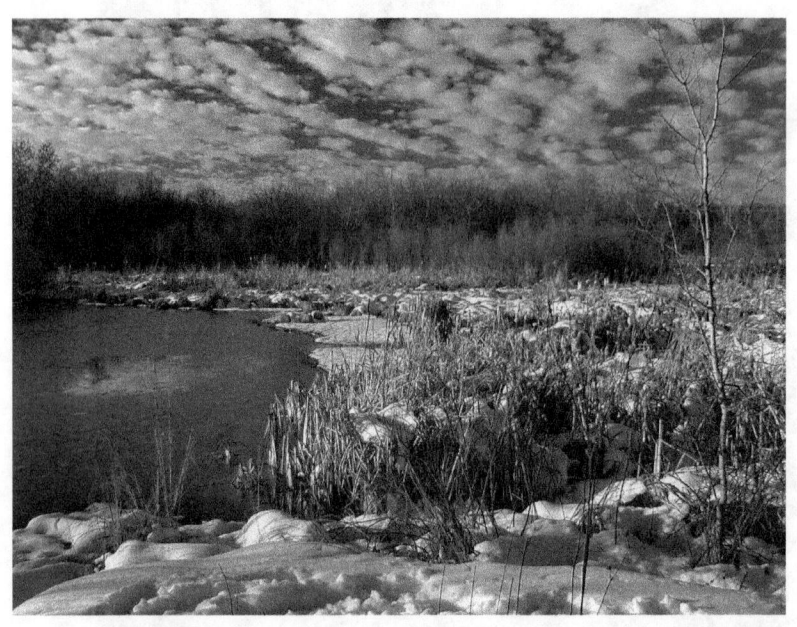

This shot is of the tower on the hill overlooking Duluth harbor in Duluth MN.

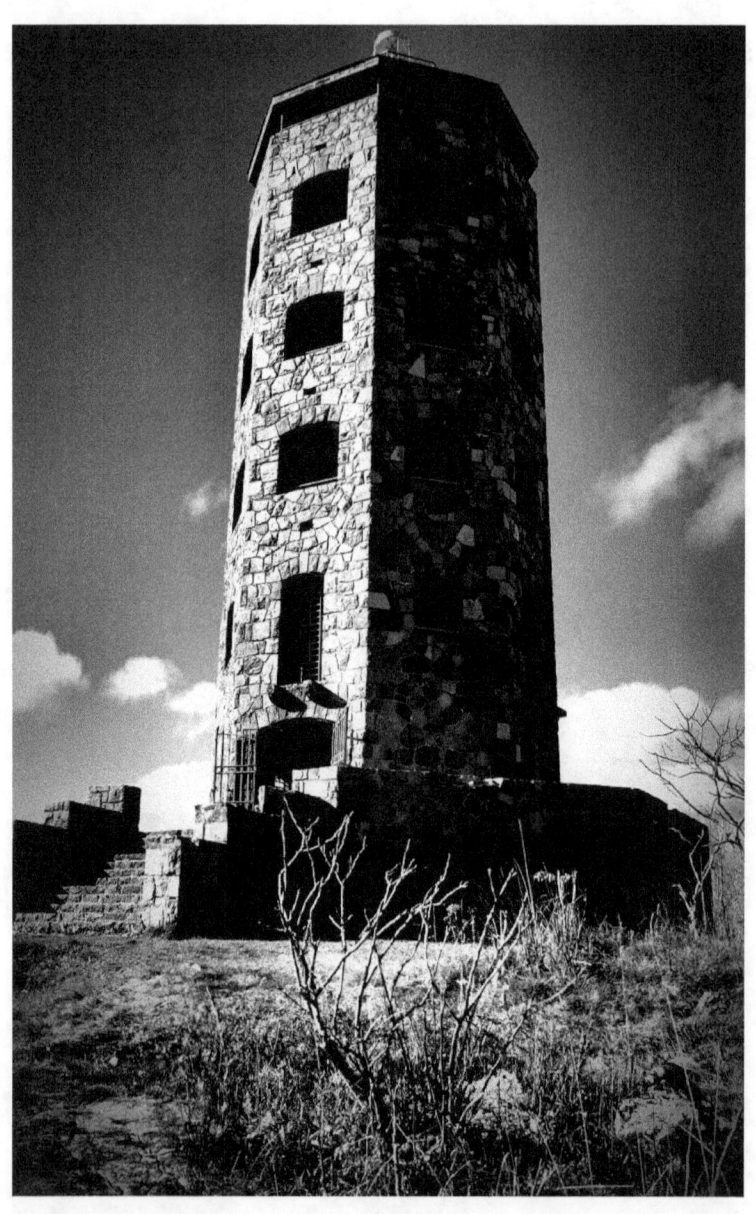

This is in the BWCA in northern MN. This is one of my all-time favorite color shots, but it also looks cool black and white.

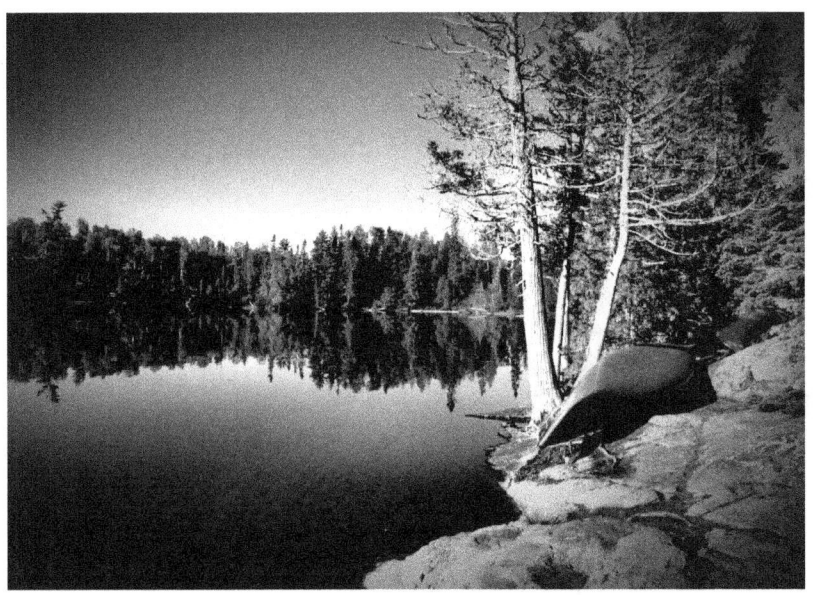

This is Palisade head on the North shore of Lake Superior.

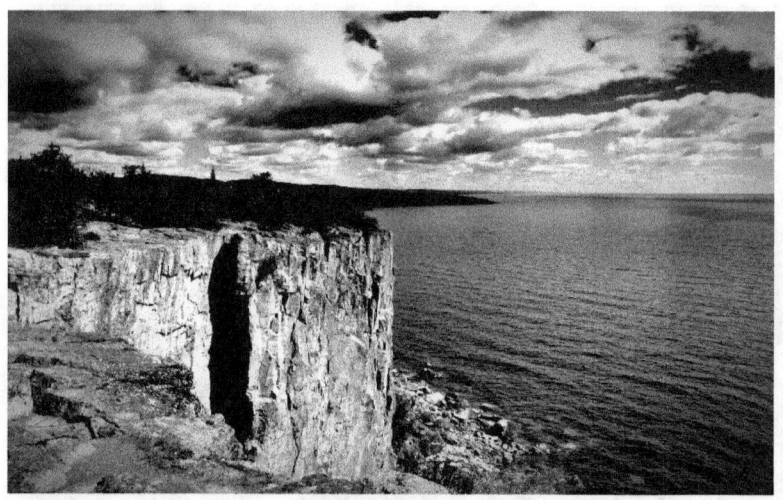

This is the Minneapolis skyline.

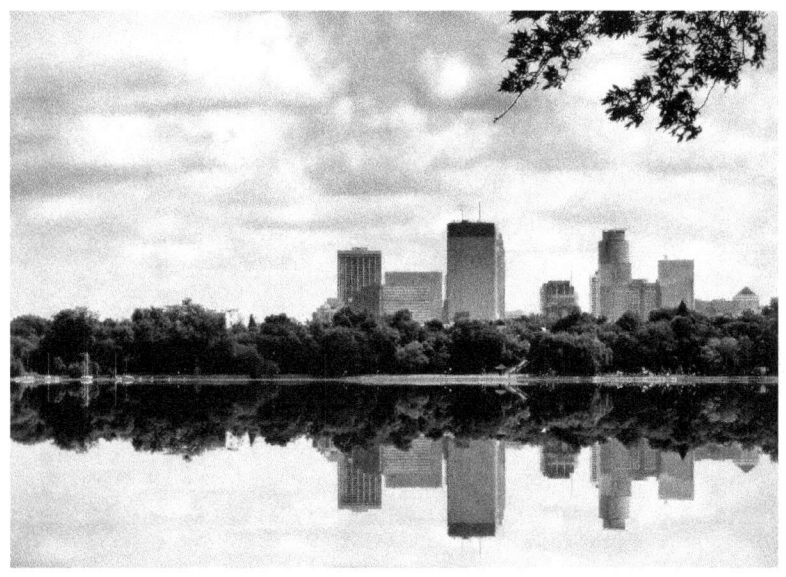

This is the famous cherry and spoon sculpture at the Minneapolis sculpture garden.

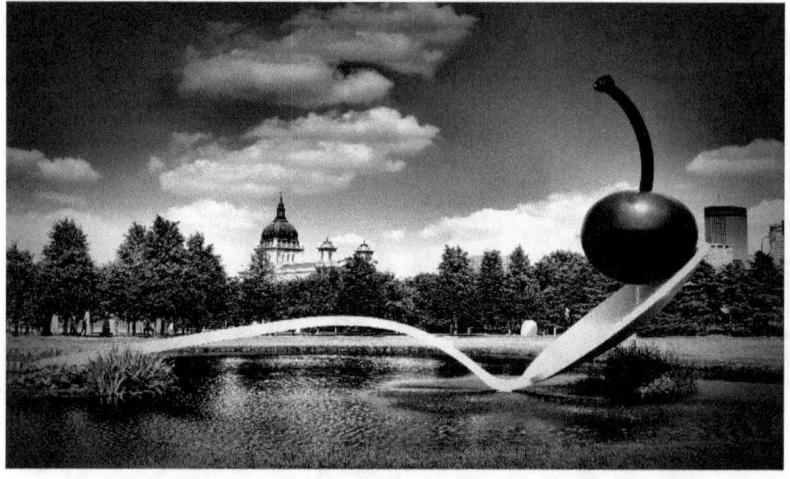

This is a shot I took from just before the unlit tunnel at Zion National Park.

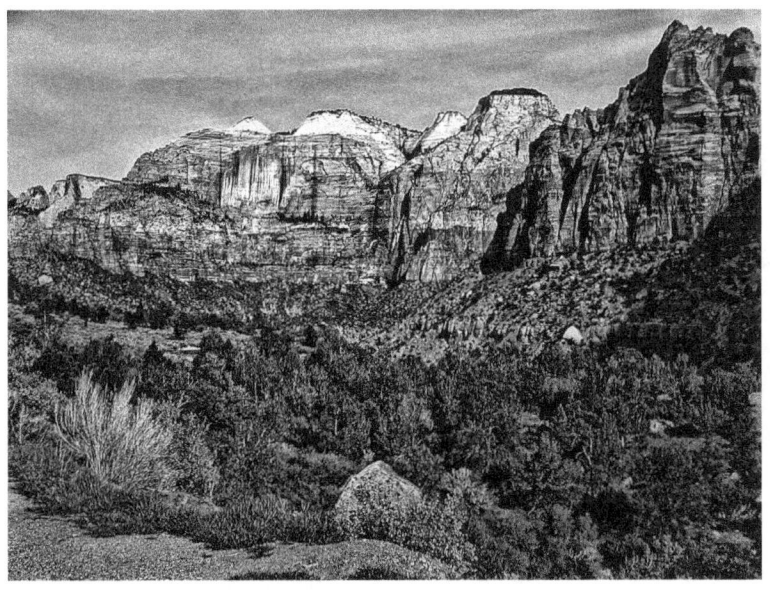

A cemetery in New Orleans.

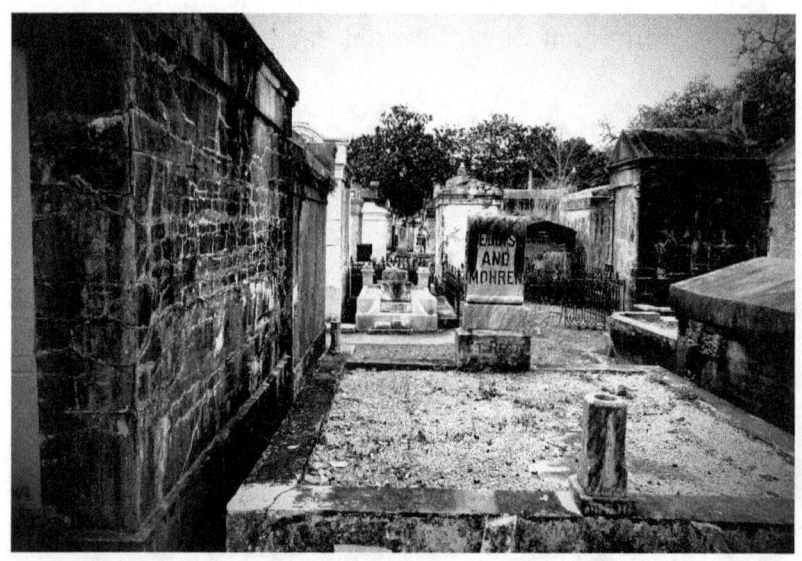

As you can see there is no limit to the shots you can create with black and white. Your creativity is the only thing that limits you with black and white.

INFRARED

Infrared photography takes you into a whole different world of black and white. I will go over digital infrared in this book. If you want to get into infrared with film, that topic is for a different book.

There are digital cameras you can use with an infrared filter and get great infrared shots. The best one I have had was an Olympus C 2100 digital camera. It took fantastic infrared shots with an infrared filter on the lens. This will give you a shot with colors that are surreal looking, and foliage is white.

I found an app for my iPhone that does a fair job of creating an infrared shot with an in-camera filter. It will help you take interesting black and white shots. One of my favorite things to do with black and white is infrared. If you have never done infrared photography, you need to check it out. The infrared filter does not look like real infrared, but it gives you a taste of what it can look like. Here is a shot I took with the infrared filter. I like it and it looks good.

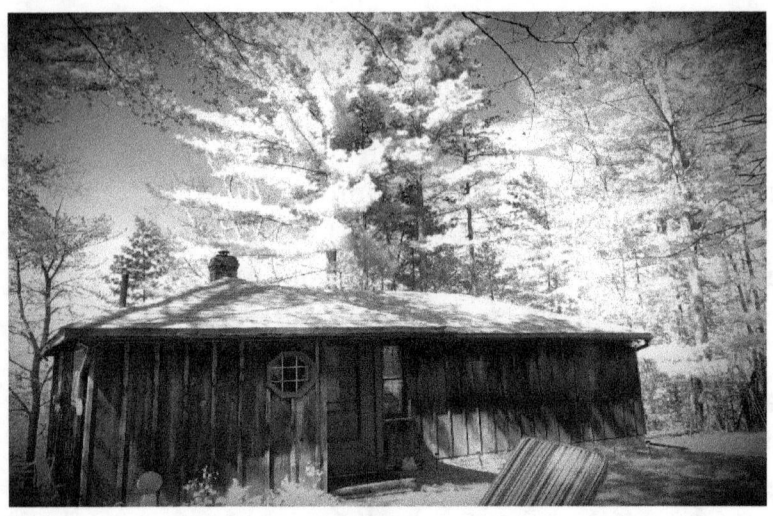

The app is great to help you see what light and shadows do to a photograph without color distraction. The app will help you get cool black and white shots even without foliage in them.

Here is a shot I took with a digital camera with an R72 infrared filter on the camera. One key to taking good infrared shots with an infrared filter is you need to have a lot of light. The filter is dark, and it blocks a lot of light. Bright sunny days at mid-day are best.

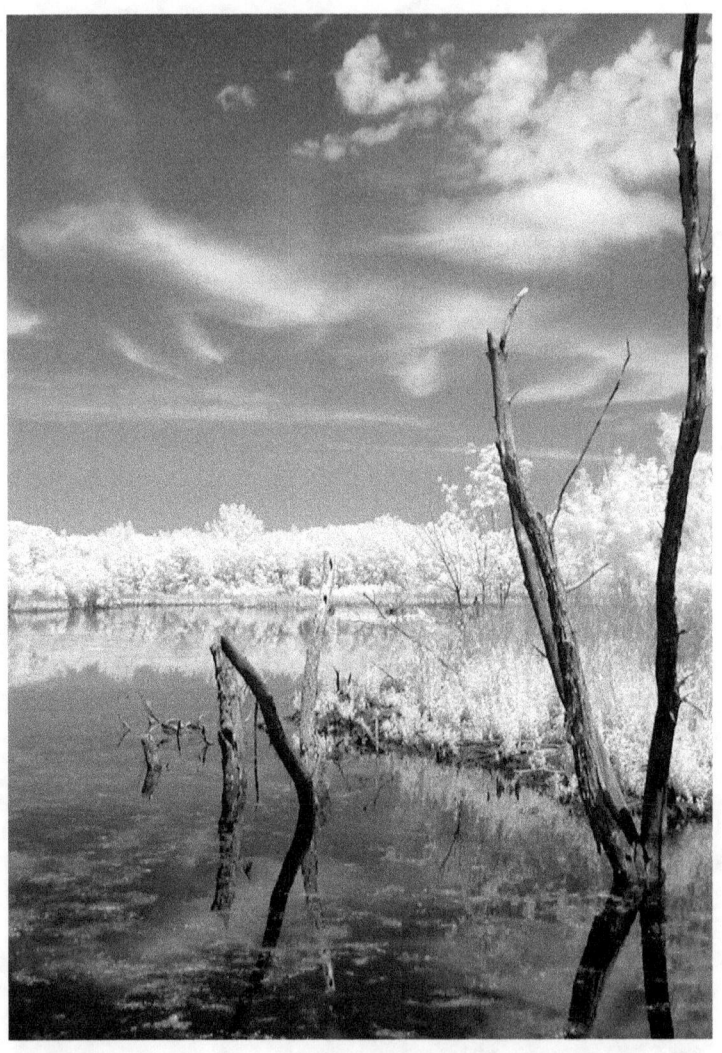

When I took the shot, it had a red tint to the whole image. I desaturated it and this is what you get. Foliage that is green turns white in infrared.

Here are a couple more I have taken. I have taken
thousands of infrared shots over the years. It gives a
surreal look that is something that looks like
nothing else. Some people may not like it, but it is
an alternate look of black and white photography.

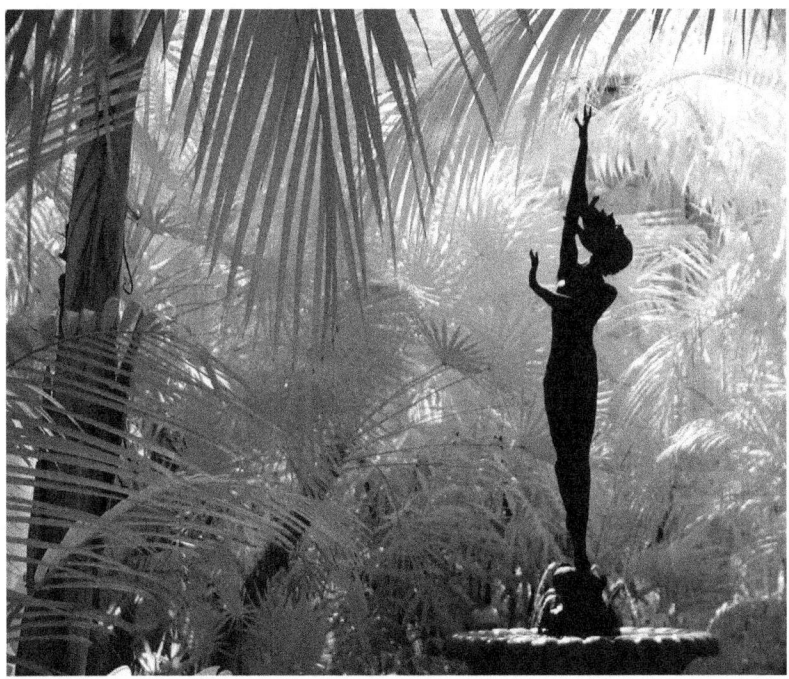

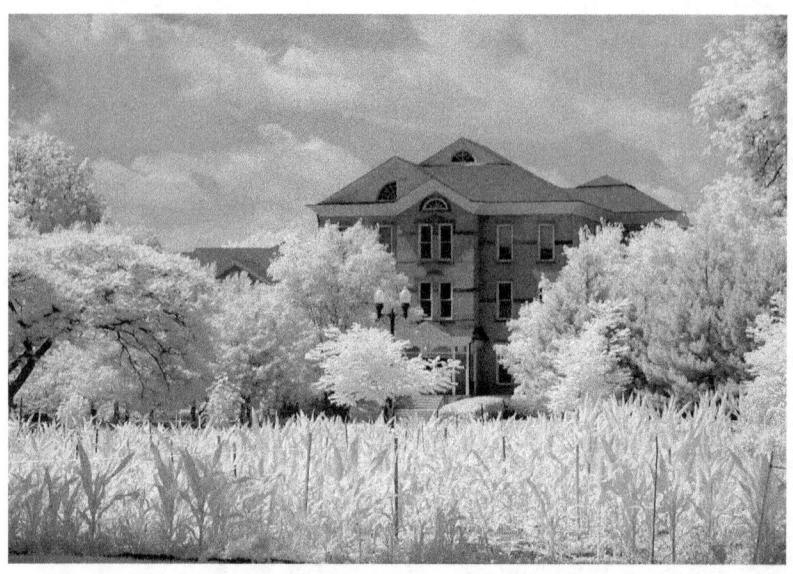

Here is what the shot looks like when it comes out
of the camera taken through the R72 filter.

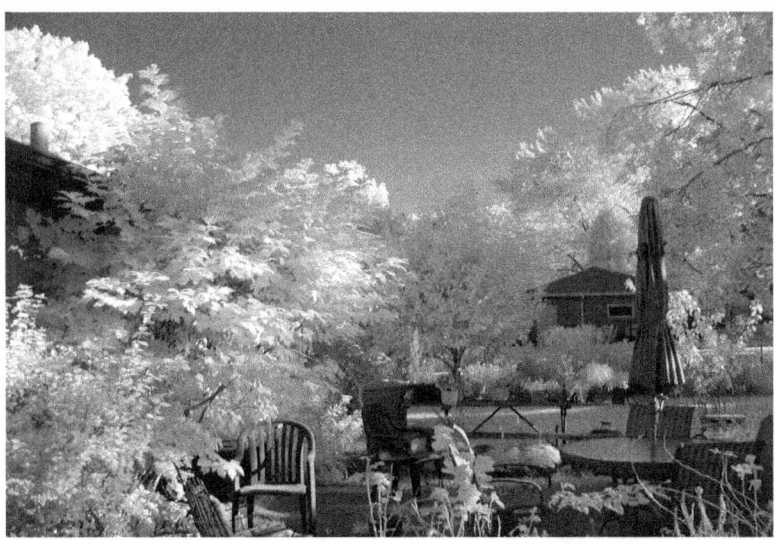

Infrared differs from any other photography. It takes practice to do it well. But it is worth the work if you want to create stunning photos like most people have never even seen before. Try it with the app or try it with a digital camera.

How to tell if your digital camera can take good infrared shots. Get an infrared remote control, look through your camera viewfinder and point the remote at the camera. If you can see the light from the remote, the camera can see infrared light. The whiter the light, the better.

Here is a shot in normal color mode, and the same shot in infrared, just for comparison.

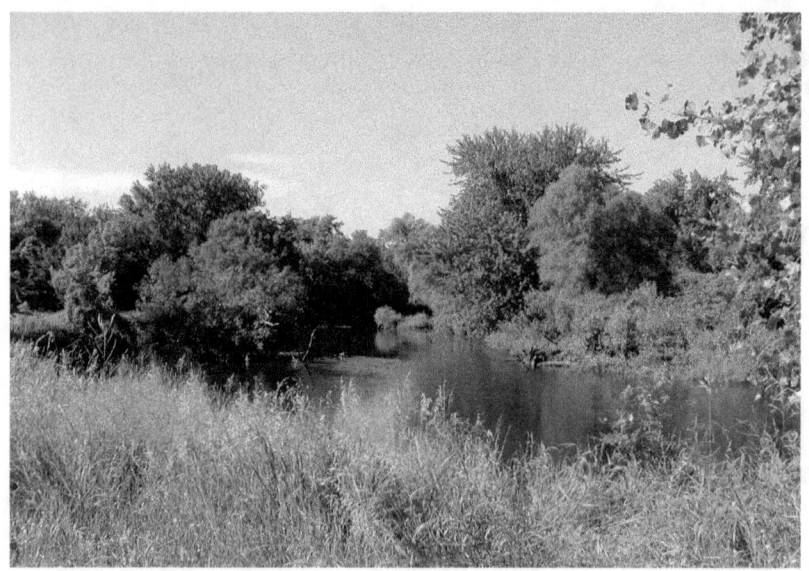

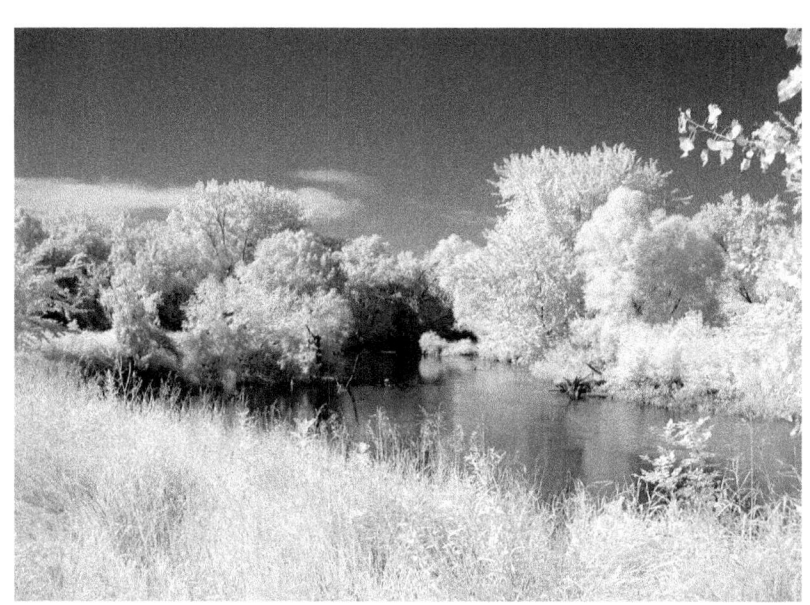

This shot is the end of Rice Creek just before it empties into the Mississippi river in Fridley MN.

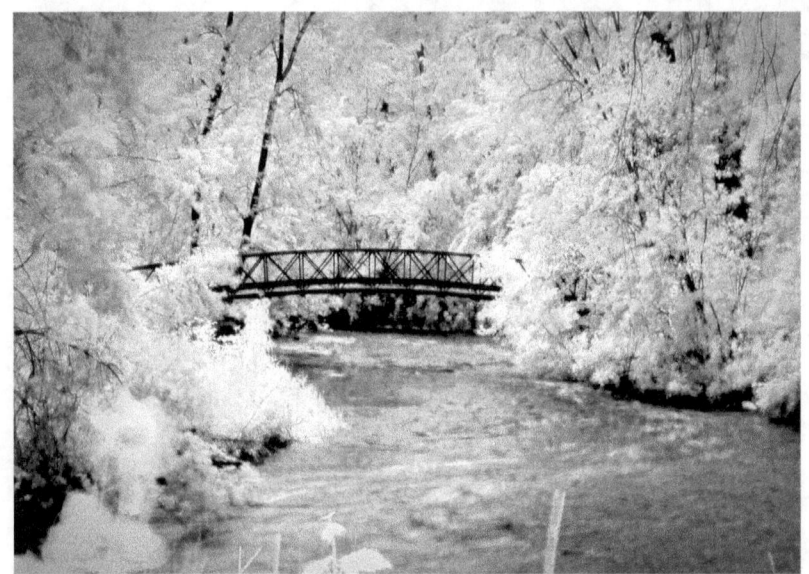

TEXTURE

Black and white photography is perfect for shots with lots of texture. Look for texture to emphasize with the contrast and tone of the black and white photos. Here is a great shot that shows what texture adds to black and white photography. It would be a cool shot without the texture, but the texture of the skin adds so much.

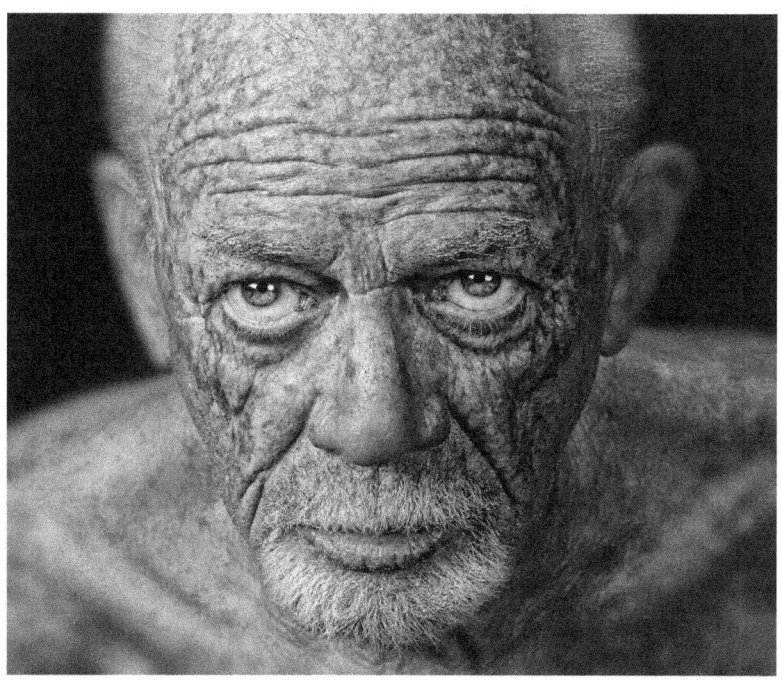

Here is another shot. I got the shot of the bee, but the texture of the wood adds to the shot.

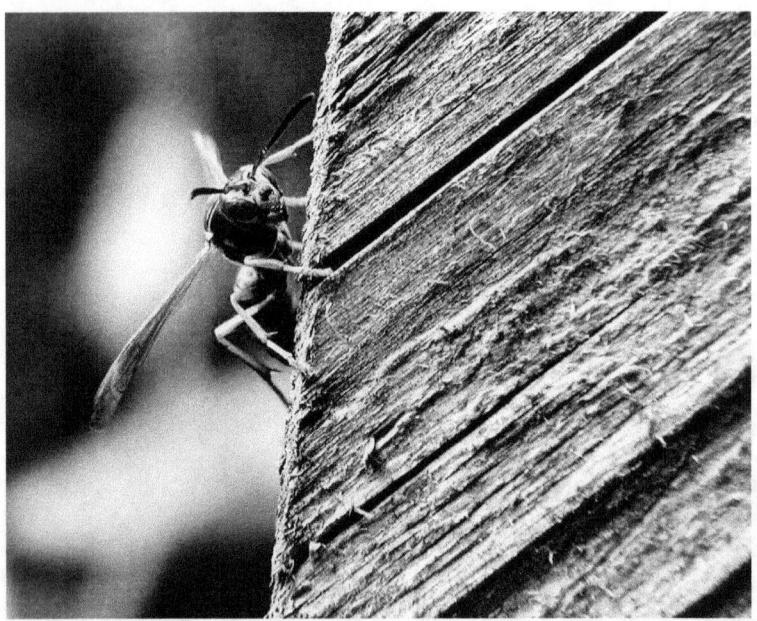

This skull is a piece I got for a photo shoot I did several years ago. Notice how the black and white draws out the texture of the skull. The skull is a foam of some type, but it looks real in black and white.

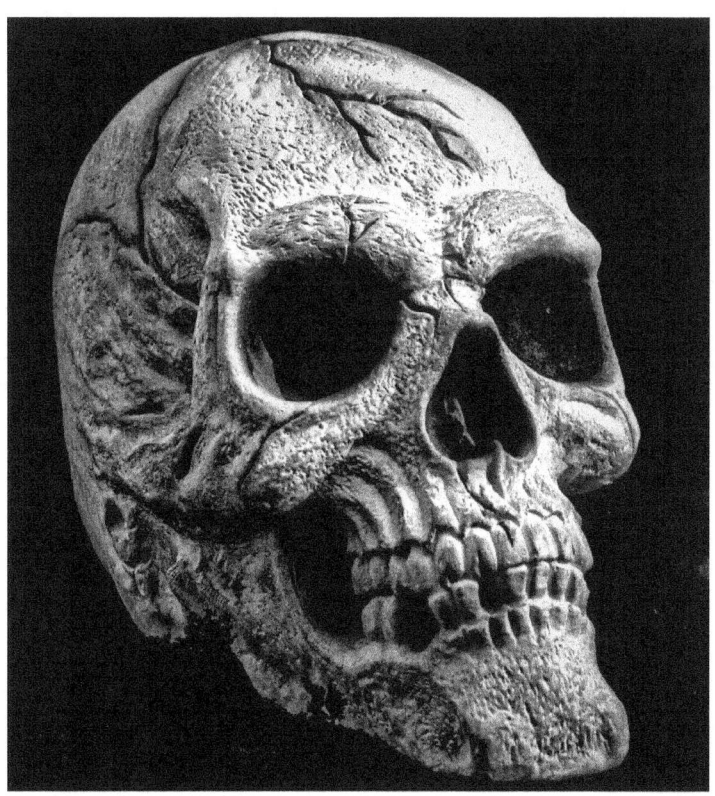

This is a great texture shot of hoar frost on some long grass.

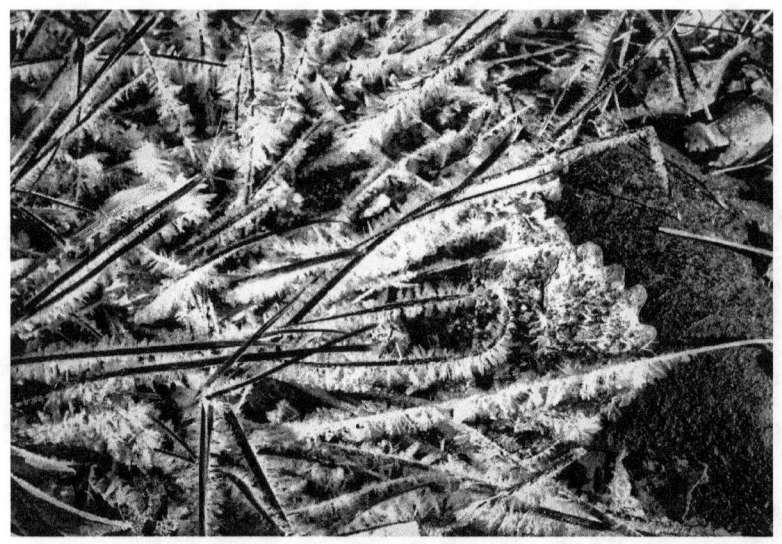

This is a pink elephant made of resin. The texture brought out by the black and white makes this a cool shot. Much better than a pink plastic elephant.

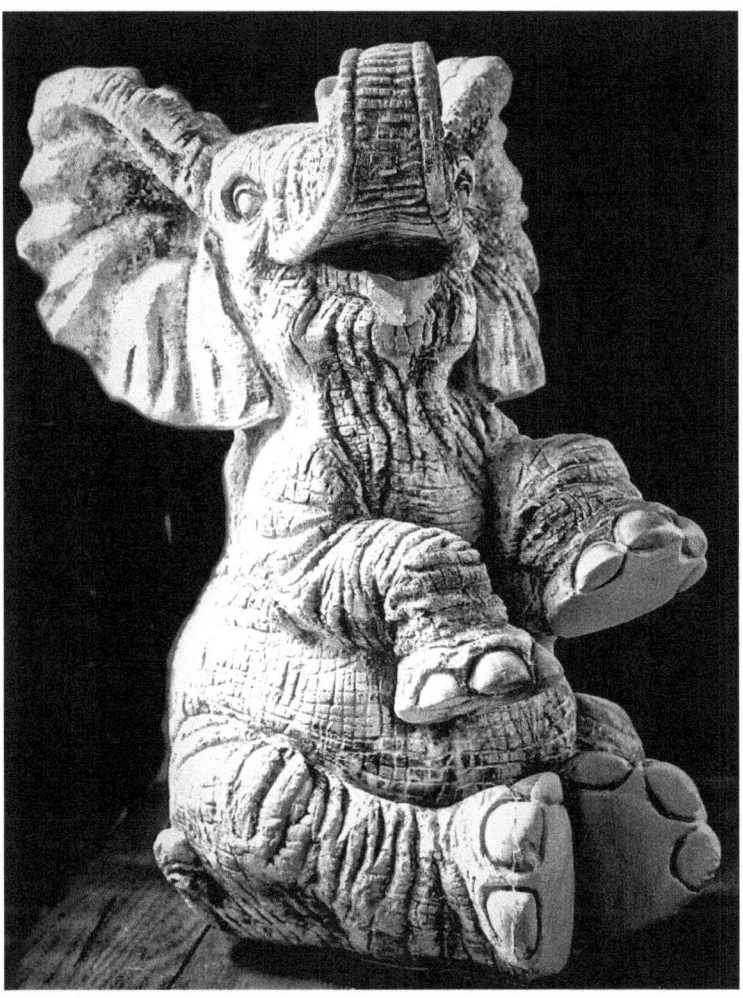

This shot is a mushroom surrounded by moss growing out of the top of a wishing well we had in the backyard.

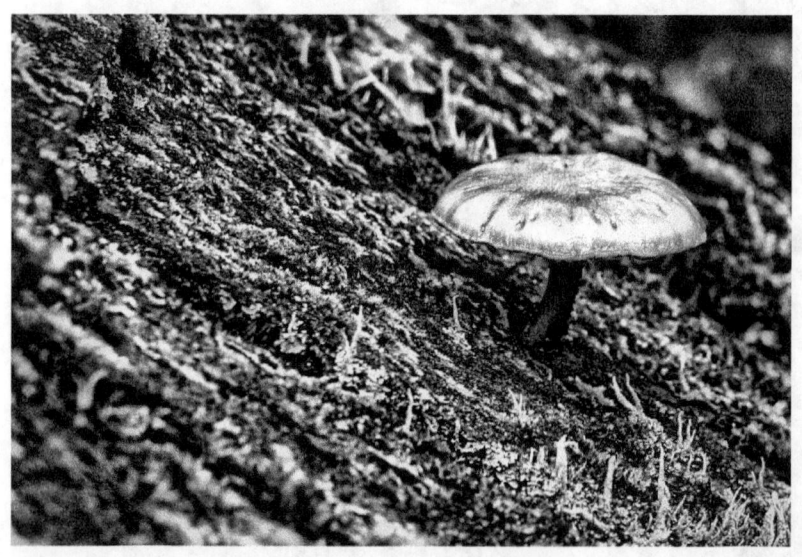

This one is to show how you can take an ordinary thing that most people would never even look at and make a cool black-and-white photo out of. Do you know what it is? It is the end of a spruce branch.

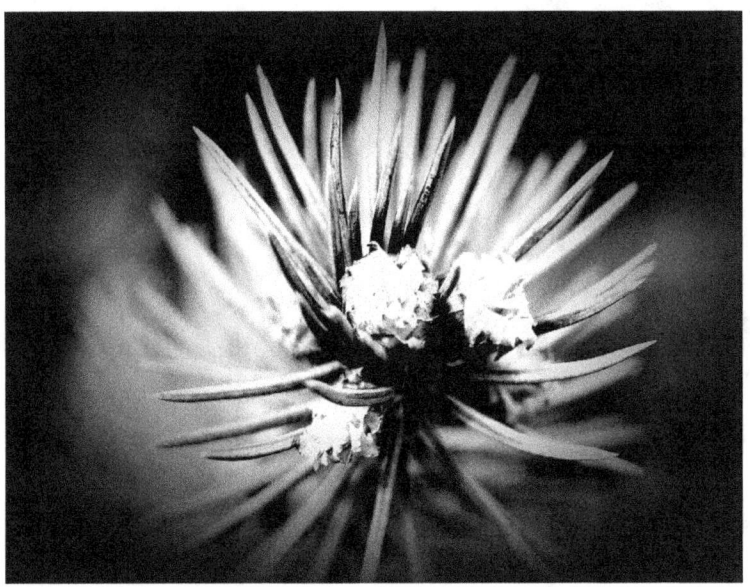

Here is a sculpture I found in Minnehaha Park. It looks cool in color also, but the black and white pulls out the texture.

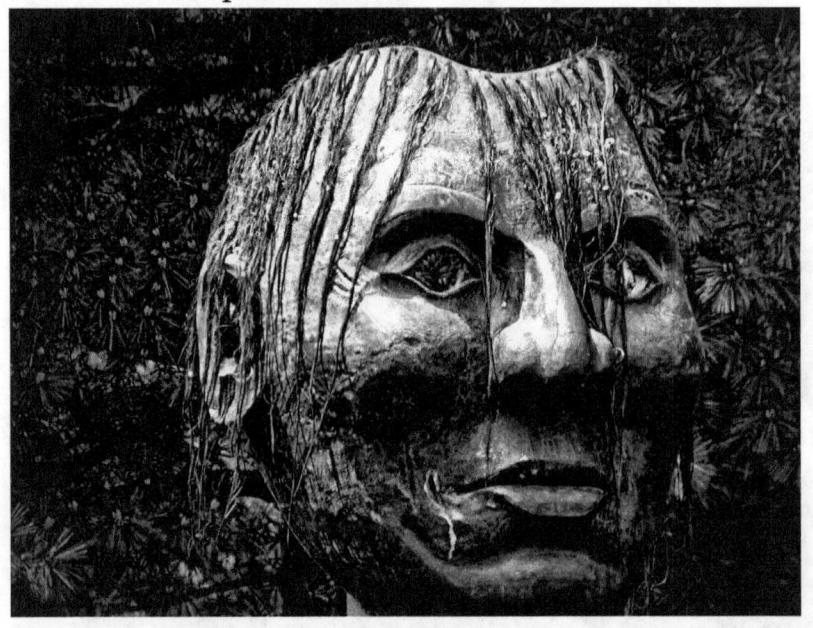

As you can see, there is so much you can do with black and white photography. The things you can do have no limits with your creativity and what you can see in the light.

PORTRAITS

Here is a great example of how full tonal contrast in a shot that goes from white to black. It shows a much more interesting photo than a color shot would. Yet the shot is still not dramatic. Will work for most portraits.

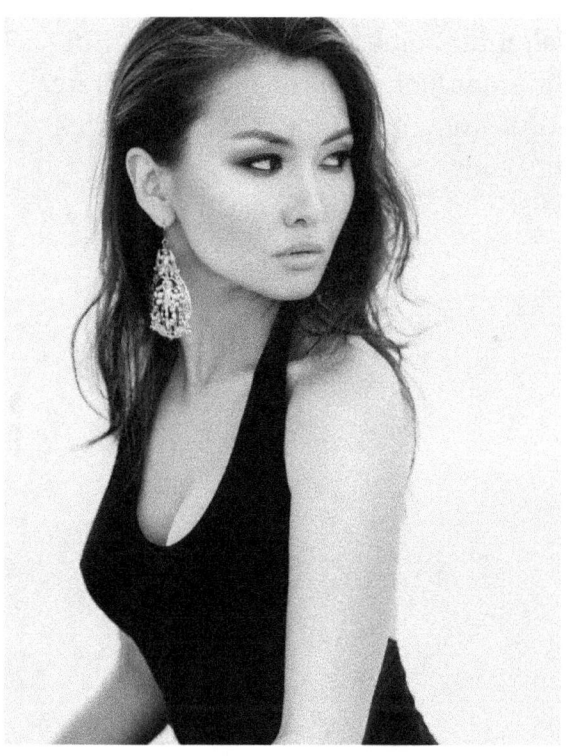

Learning to see the tonal contrast when shooting black and white will also make you a better color photographer. It will make you look more at the light and look more at the shadows in the scene.

Most portraits that look good will also look good in black and white. Some portraits that look ok will look fantastic in black and white. The texture shot above is a good example. The high key shot in the selective color section with blue eyes is another example of a shot that looks good either way. But has a touch different look with the blue eyes. Here is just a beautiful woman that looks terrific in this black and white shot.

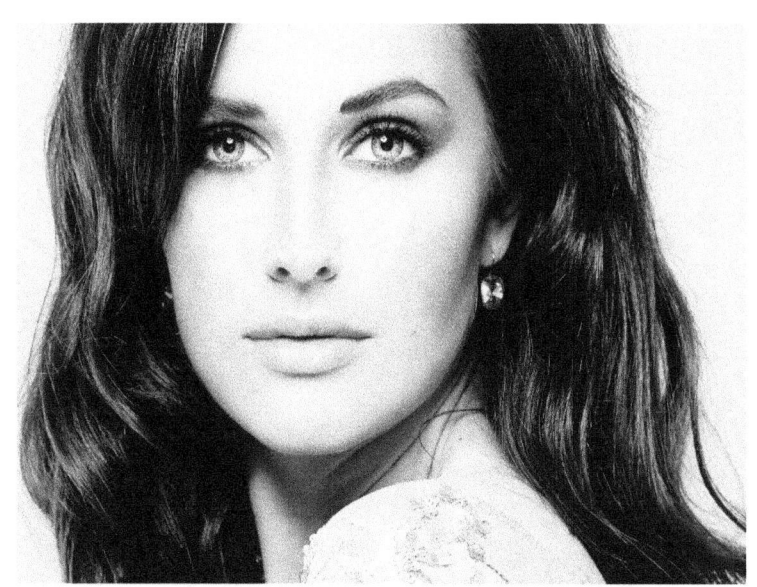

Here is a portrait I made with black and white with a cobalt look. Another cool variation.

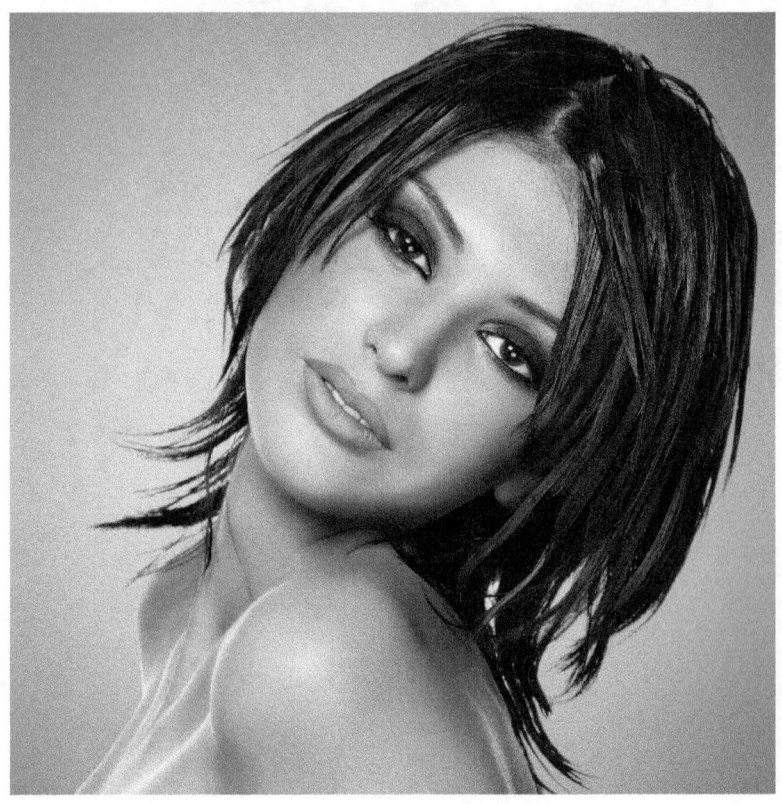

This is a shot I took at the zoo. The gorilla was only a few feet away behind thick glass. He gave me a look I could not pass up. What do you think he was thinking? This shot was not great. There was a reflection from the glass and where I was shooting from is dark. I shot this with a f1.8 50mm lens with a shutter speed of 1/20 handheld. In color I was disappointed. Black and white, I like it.

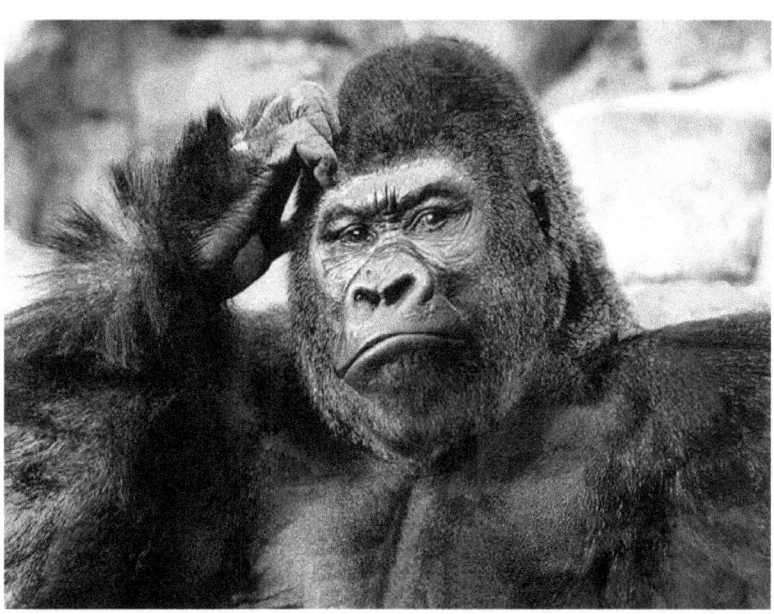

This shot done with little more than desaturating.
Just did a little darkening in the spots it needed
around the eyes.

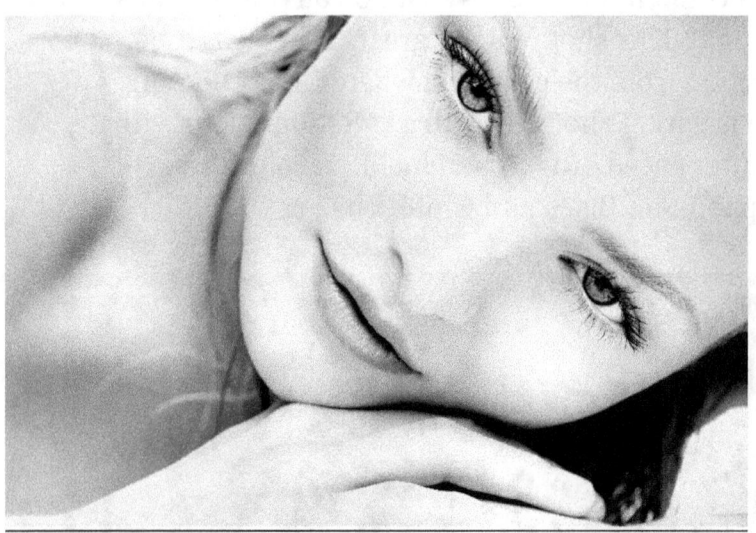

This portrait shows how the light and shadows make a big difference.

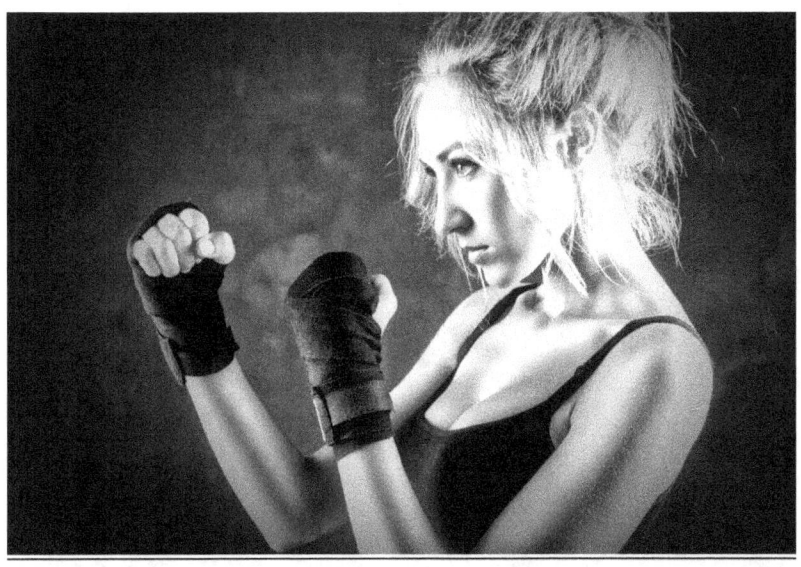

Here is a cool Silhouette. The shot was color and I converted it too black-and-white. It is even cooler in black-and-white.

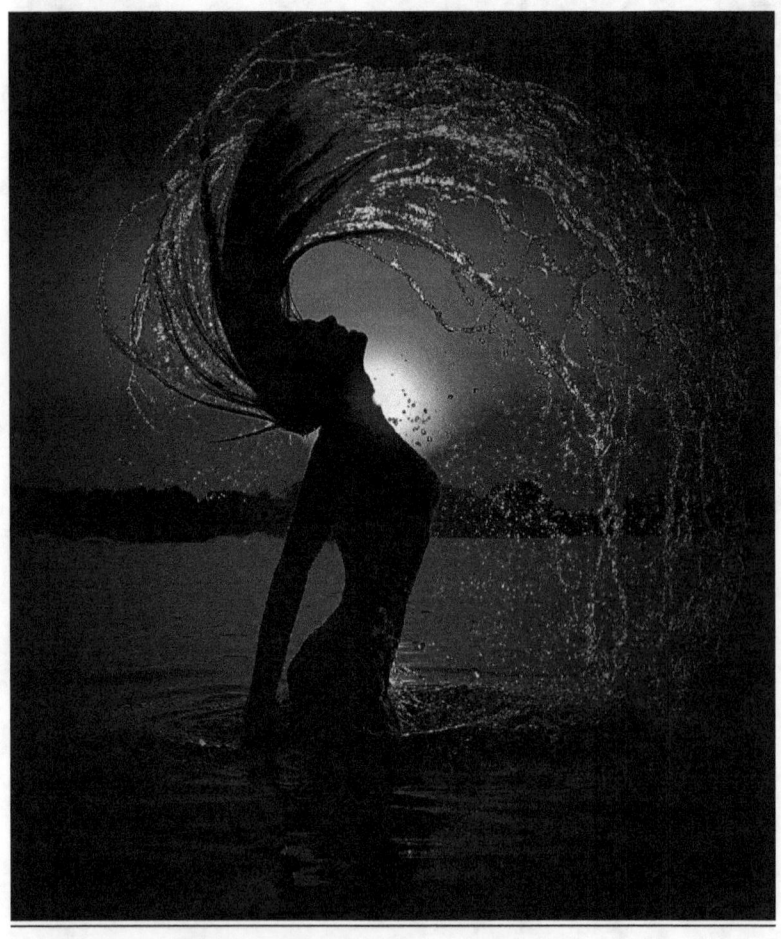

One last example of what you can do with black and white portraits. I like both shots, but the black and white looks more powerful and more interesting. What do you think?

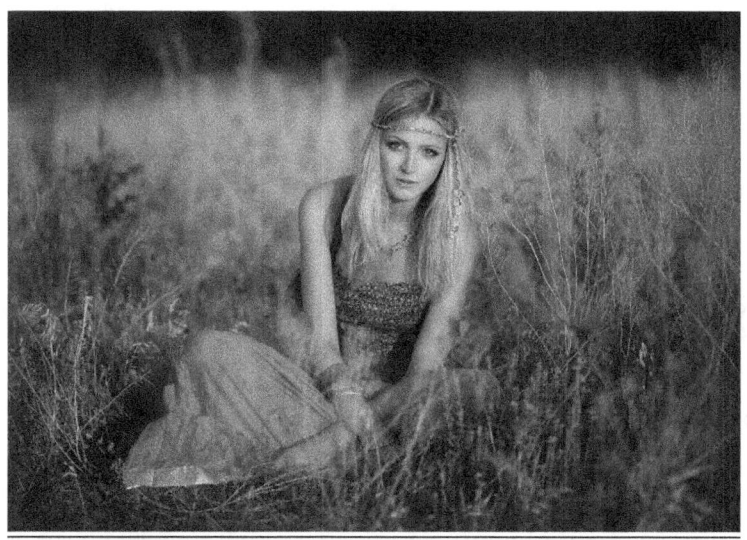

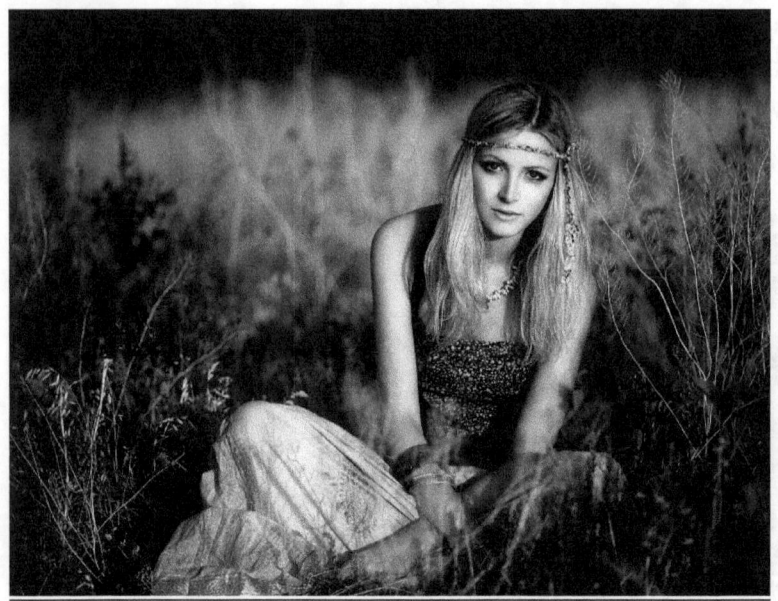

As you can see, portraits also can often be made better in black and white. You can get almost any look you want with a little work and imagination.

HIGH KEY BLACK AND WHITE PORTRAIT

High key images look great with the right shot. Some of them are stunning even though there is not much detail in the shot. You need a good portrait with a good face shot that is sharp and focused on the eyes. A light background also helps.

- Open the image you want to use.
- Copy the image.
- Crop to have just the parts you want in the shot.
- Desaturate the image.
- Duplicate layer and blend using screen.
- Open the curves tool and set it close to this.

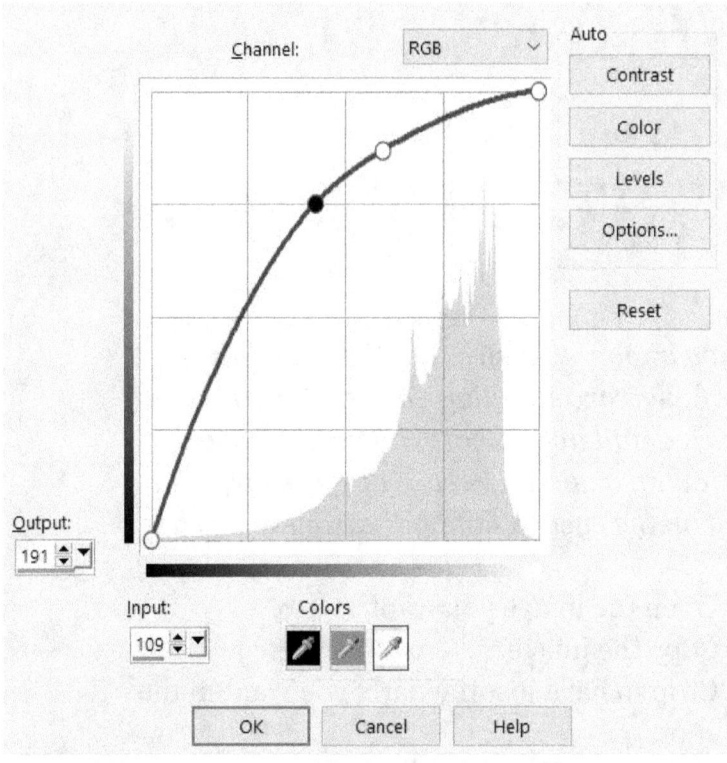

- Flatten layers and merge down.
- Duplicate the adjusted layer.
- Apply Gaussian blur to the top layer, a radius of 18 to 20 pixels.
- Then go to the top layer and in the blend, mode select overlay.
- Adjust the opacity down a bit.

- Pick the burn tool and burn around the eyes and mouth until you get the look you are going for.
- Use the dodge tool to lighten any areas you want lighter.
- Merge down and flatten.
- Duplicate layer again.
- Play with the blend mode. I like to darken, or multiply.
- Adjust amount to get the perfect look you want.

Starting color image

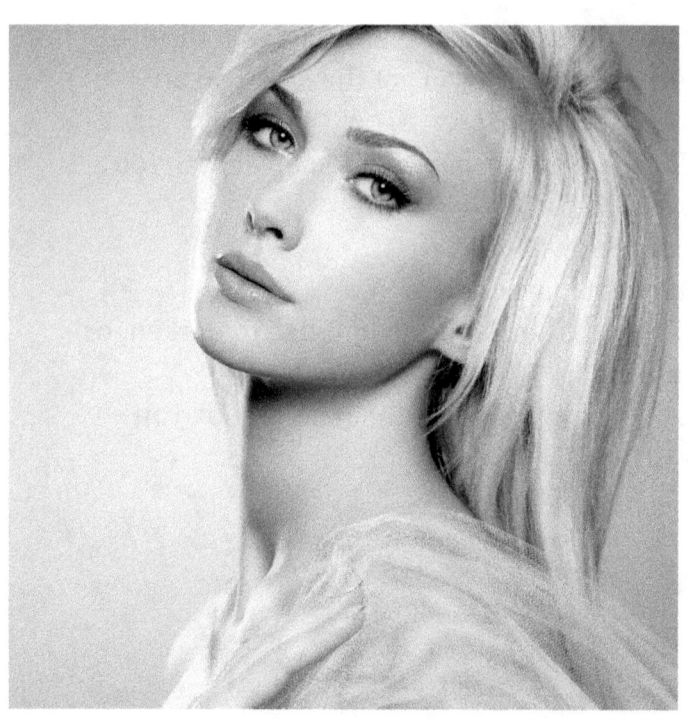

High Key image

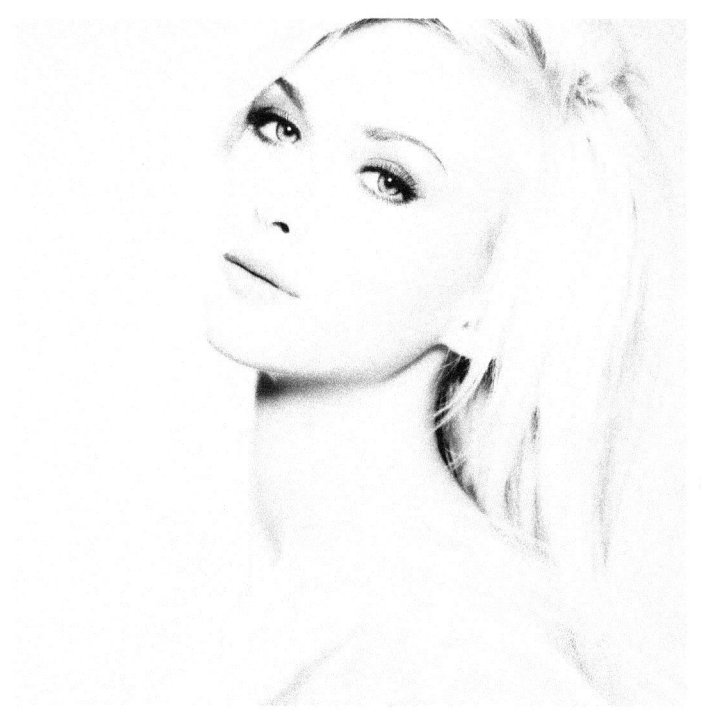

As you can see, she is stunning either way, but the high key a different look. Different mood and different impression.

Here is another example done with the instructions above.

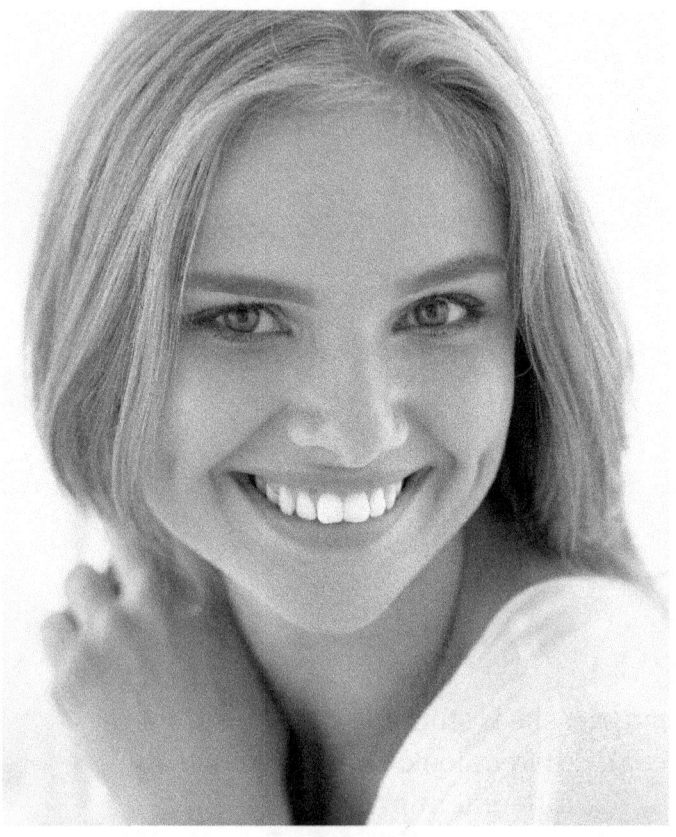

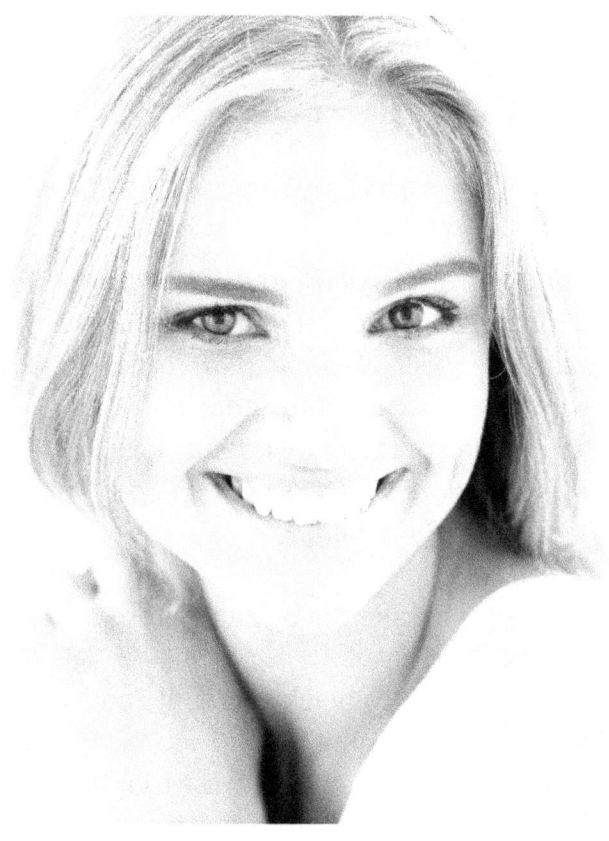

As you can see there is nothing wrong with the color versions of these shots. The high key gives a quite different mood and different look for the right application.

USING SELECTIVE COLOR

This is something you see a lot of now. One reason is because it shows creativity and can add much to the shot. You can use this technique in all forms of photography to make cool-looking shots. Selective color is easy to do. One of the huge advantages of selective color is that your viewers eyes will go straight to the subject of the photo.

- The best way is to take the original shot.
- Make a duplicate layer.
- Adjust the top layer to black and white and get the look you are going for.
- Then just zoom in and use an erase tool to erase the top layer in the area where you want the color to show through.
- Then just merge the layers and flatten and you are done.

Here is a portrait I did with the steps I listed, and it looks cool. Her blue eyes add just a touch of color to the high key shot. You can do something subtle like

this shot, or you can do something dramatic. Like
the shot of the bike.

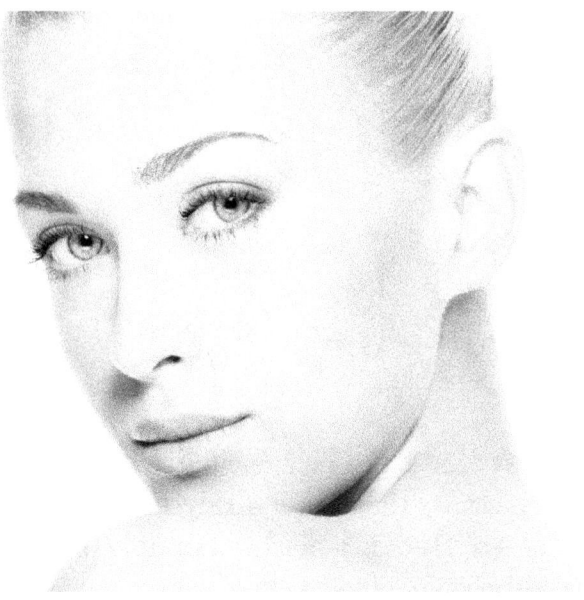

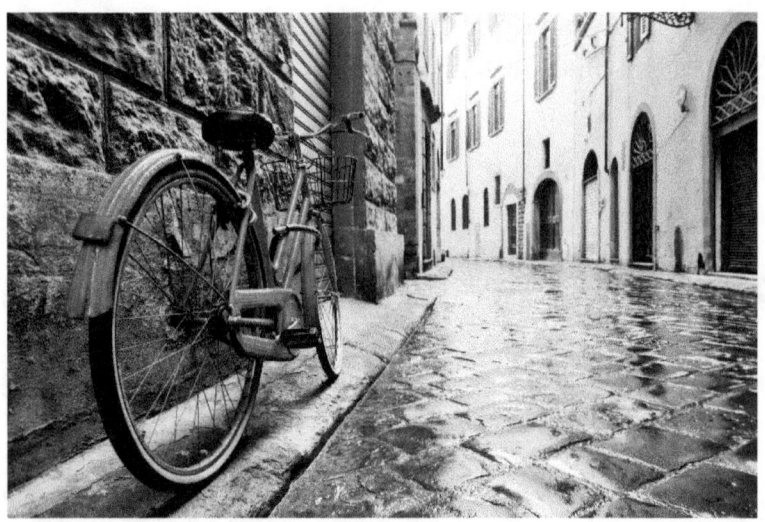

Selective color is fun because it gives a very distinct look and draws the viewer straight to the subject guaranteed. Here is a perfect example of the power of selective color. In the shot below, what is the first thing your eyes go too? If the photo were all color, the first thing you would see is the girl. Using the selective color, the first thing you see is the flag. This is just to show you the power of this method of photography.

Selective color photos can be great for some things, they emphasize specific subjects. Use them for the right things and people will love them.

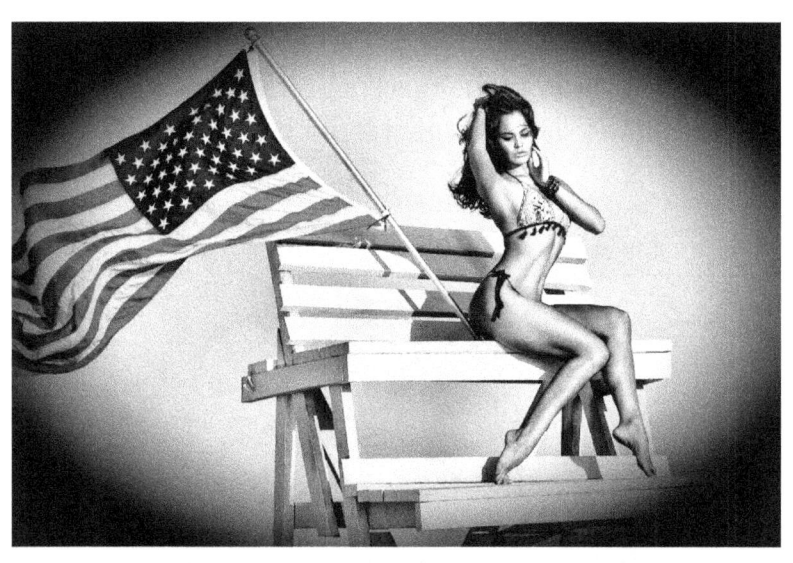

Here is one more selective color shot I made. The shot is good in color, but in black and white with the red left in the shot. I think it looks better.

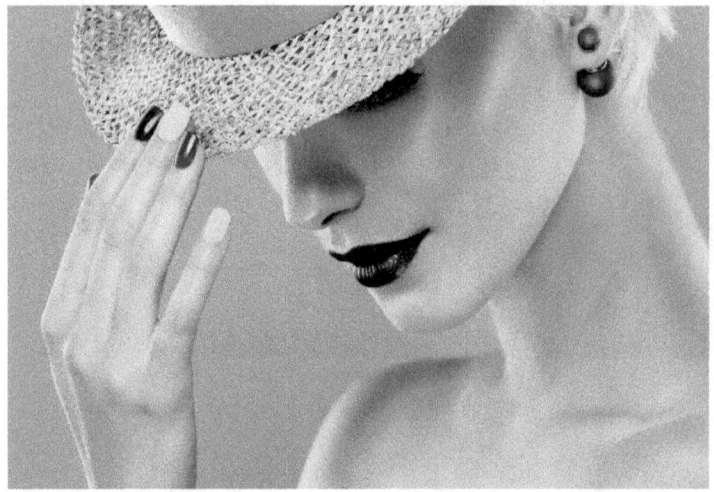

Selective color is another form of black and white you can have a lot of fun with.

PHONE CAMERA APPS

Some of the best black and white conversions are available on apps on your phone. If you want to learn to see the best looks, convert to black and white with phone apps. I have 3 favorite apps I use.

One of my favorites is Enlight for converting. My favorites for shooting black and white with your phone are apps called black cam and Dramatic black and white. Black cam costs $1.99 but is well worth the cost if you want to see the shot in black and white. It lets you use filters on the shot to see what the photo will look like as you take it. Dramatic costs $4.99, well worth it. You can make the same shots with the apps, but it takes work in a photo editor.

Here is a shot I took at the cabin using the black cam app. It can take a boring picture and subject and makes it an interesting shot. Just because of the tones and the big contrast.

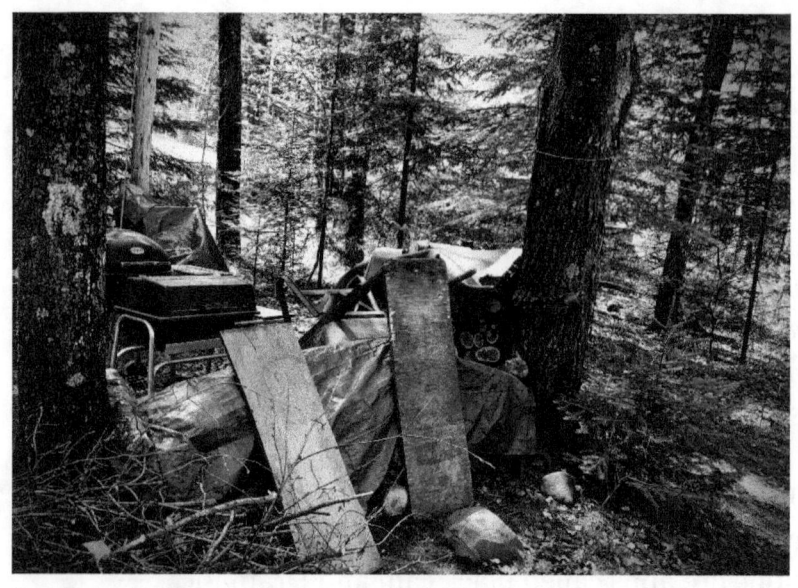

Argentum camera is another black and white app that is useful. This one is free. It does a good job with black and white shots. The best thing about these apps is that it lets you see the scene and compose it without the color distracting from what you see. It has the fewest features, but it is free.

These are the 2 best apps I have found for taking shots in black and white.

The best apps for converting color shots to black and white.

Black Cam, the app I mentioned above that lets you take shots in black and white, will also let you import shots you did not take in the app, and lets you adjust them in the app.
Tap the little landscape looking thing on the lower left and it will take you to your camera roll and let you bring pictures into the app.

Dramatic black and white. This is the other app I would recommend. One of the big differences between the apps is the dramatic black and white use of your camera app on your phone. It is a cool option with the iPhone plus, you can use all the cool camera features of the iPhone plus. This app also lets you use pictures and convert them that were not take with the app. If I had to have only one, this would be the one.

Here is a shot I converted to black and white with dramatic black and white.

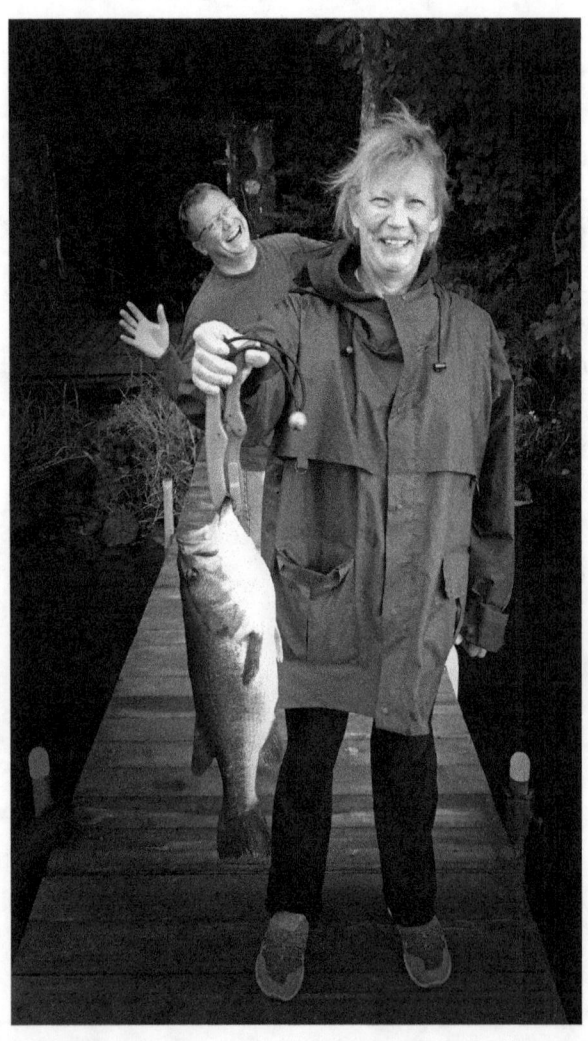

From the park at Minnehaha falls.

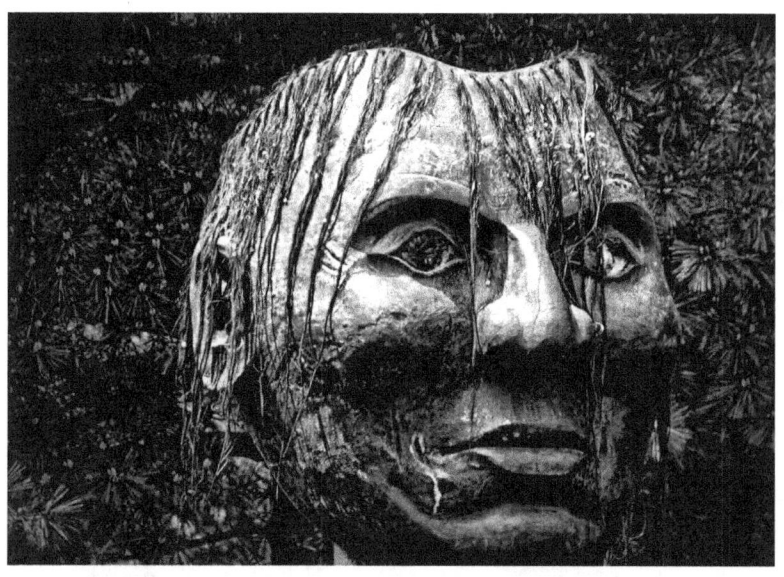

An ore ship in Lake Superior. This shot was taken with a long zoom. The ship was a long way out. It came out great.

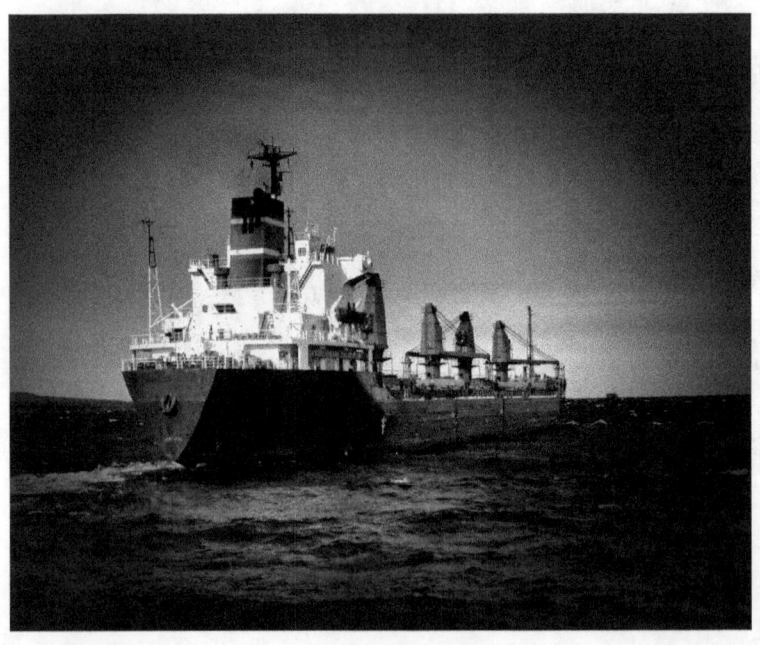

A cool old tractor from a show I went too many years ago.

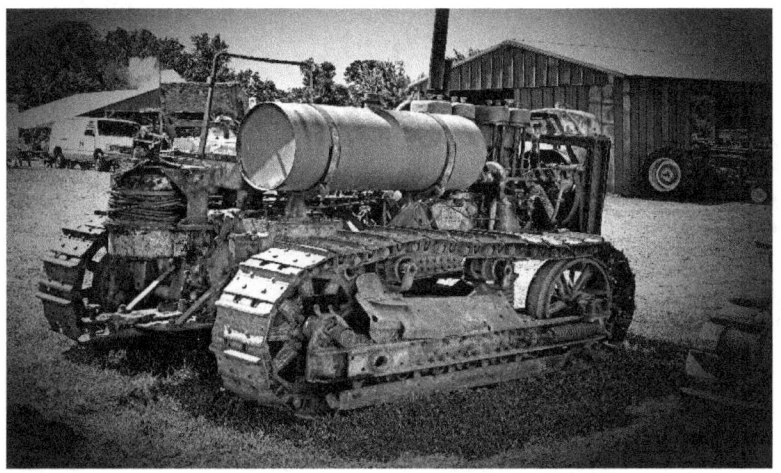

Here is another cool tractor from the same show.

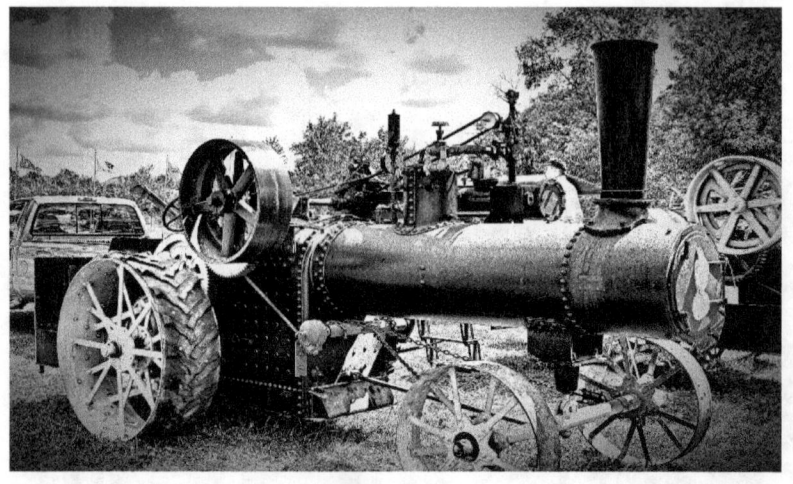

A cool cabin or old farmhouse.

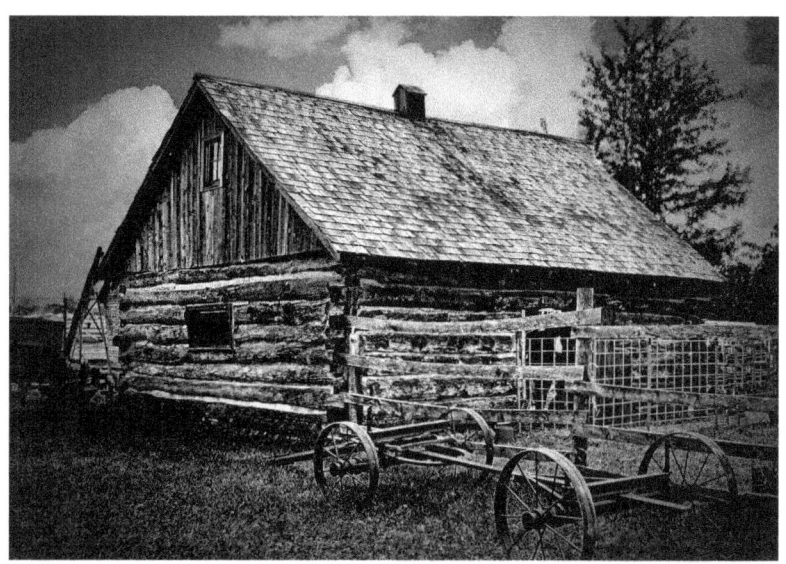

PRINTING

You can print your own black and white prints and they will look good if you have a great print to work with. One thing I have found is if you want to have outstanding black and white prints, it is best to get them printed from one of the online printers that specialize in black and white.

My favorite is **Mpix**. They can do a metallic printing paper or a true black and white paper that will give you the best print by far. You can print your own and they will look ok. If you want them to look great, have the pro's print them for you. You will not regret doing it.

Not all shots will look good in the metallic, but some are breathtaking. Order some metallics so you can see what they look like. Do a comparison to see what looks best for your type of print.

WRAP IT UP

Cool things about shooting great black and white photos. With the technology we have now, you do not even need an SLR camera. You can make great black and white photos with a phone camera now. There are also some great pocket cameras on the market that work well for black and white. This is now something anyone who likes to take great photos can do.

There are many things you can shoot in black and white that will be great shots. There are many ways of converting to black and white. Most of them are easy to do. It is much easier now than it was a few years ago. You do not have to be a photoshop master to make great black and white photos.

You can use color filters on your film camera, or digital. The different color filters give you a different look, it all depends on what you like and what you want. You can make great portraits with black and white. You can make high key black and white shots that look cool, or you can make low key shots that are dark and moody. You can also do everything in between.

You can make shots with selective color that leave pieces of color in the shot to give it a different look and will draw the viewer's eyes where you want them to look.

You can use your phone camera to do many awesome shots. With digital you can practice as much as you want for no cost. If you do not like it, delete it. Try different things to your shots. Retake them, whatever you want to do. There is no limit to what you can do with digital.

When I started taking the art of photography seriously, digital was not around for the average person. Shooting black and white in film was a lot of guesswork and I took many rolls of film that were not great shots. You can still do it that way, but digital is great.

If you like the look of black and white and you want to make cool shots, get out there and shoot and convert to black and white and make people say WOW.

I would appreciate it if you would take a minute and go to the Amazon site and leave a review for this book. Also check out my website with links to my

other books. Thanks again for reading my book.
http://www.stevepease.net

ABOUT ME

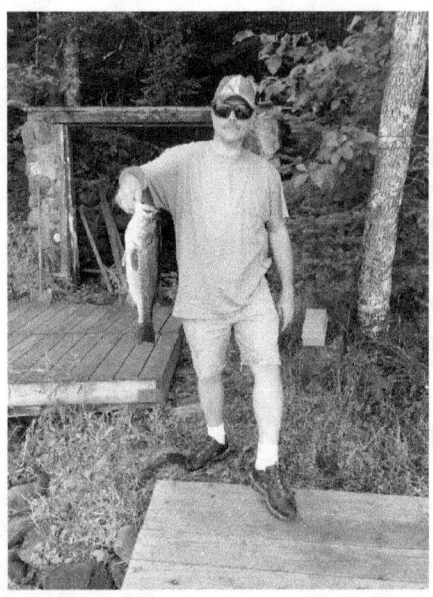

My name is Steve Pease. I live in the Northern suburbs of the Twin Cities in Minnesota.

I have been writing for about eight years. I have written several hundred articles for Hub Pages and for the examiner over the years. For Examiner I wrote a column for the Twin Cities on Disc golf, and one on Cycling in the Twin Cities, and one on Exercise and fitness for the Twin cities.

I write on subjects I am passionate about, disc golf, exercise, photography, cycling, fishing, and topics that deal with Christian beliefs.

My father is a retired minister, and he has written many books. I have edited many of them and have them available on my site that cover many topics of interest to Christians today. I have also written an Old Testament trivia book on my own.

 I have been playing disc golf since 1978 and love the sport. The greatest thing about disc golf is at age sixty-three I am still extremely competitive and beat players much younger than me. Disc golf is a sport you can play at almost any age if you can walk.

I have taken several hundred thousand pictures over the last 35 years and I am always trying to improve my photography. My goal is always to take the best shots I can. I want people to say wow when they look at my shots. I went through the photography course at New York Institute of photography many years ago. What I learned from the course and my years of experience was worth every dollar.

The key to be a great photographer is to see things that most people do not see, or in a way they did not see it. My favorite types of photography are landscape, portrait, animals and infrared. I have shot several weddings and spend hundreds of hours just exploring different places looking for great things to take pictures of.

I have been an avid fisherman since I was a kid. I have had 2 bass fishing boats over the years, but I enjoy fishing from my kayak. I have an old town kayak, and a sit on top feelfree Moken 12 fishing kayak. I also have two old town canoes for going to the boundary waters wilderness area or just paddling around lakes in my area.

 The hardest part about fishing from a kayak is trying to decide what not to take with me. As with most bass fishermen, I have tons of equipment, and I always feel I need to take it all with me, just in case. Kayak fishing has made me downsize just to make everything fit in my kayak.

I spend most of my <u>fishing time catching bass and northern pike</u>. But if I am looking for a good meal, you cannot beat crappies and sunfish. I have spent most of my time fishing freshwater, but I have caught saltwater fish. The biggest was a 380-pound bull shark off Key West Florida in 1985.

I have also loved biking and exercising since I was in my early teens. I like to read nonfiction books so I can keep learning new things all the time. Many of the things I learn I want to share with you and help enrich your life. I want to pass on the knowledge I have learned over the years and share it with others.

Thanks again.

Check out my book site for other good books.
<u>Stevepease. net</u>

OTHER BOOKS YOU MAY BE INTERESTED IN

Learn to take great photos with your phone camera

CAMERA PHONE
HOW TO TAKE GREAT PHOTOS
WITH YOUR PHONE AND TABLET

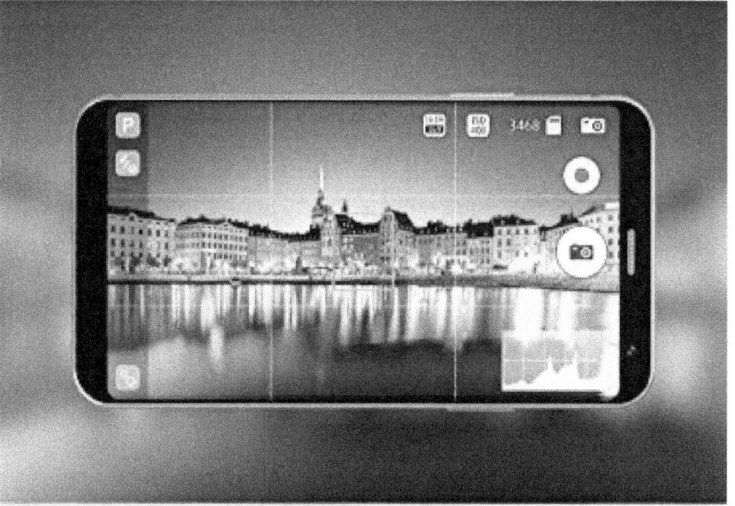

TIPS TO MAKE YOU
A GREAT PHOTOGRAPHER

Steve Pease

You are with your friends and something memorable is happening and you want to capture it so you take pictures you will want to keep as memories. You get home and upload them to your computer so you can post process them. Or just check them out. And maybe you will get prints made. But your photos are blurry. Not terrible, but not good enough to print.

You have pictures you can save for memories on your phone, but they look terrible any bigger. Taking great pictures with a phone camera is harder than with a DSLR. A lot of the reason is that the iPhone is lighter, which makes it harder to hold still, and you are likely taking those types of pictures while having fun, and not thinking about taking pictures.

<u>Landscape photography. Learn to shoot great landscapes by doing projects that teach you how.</u>

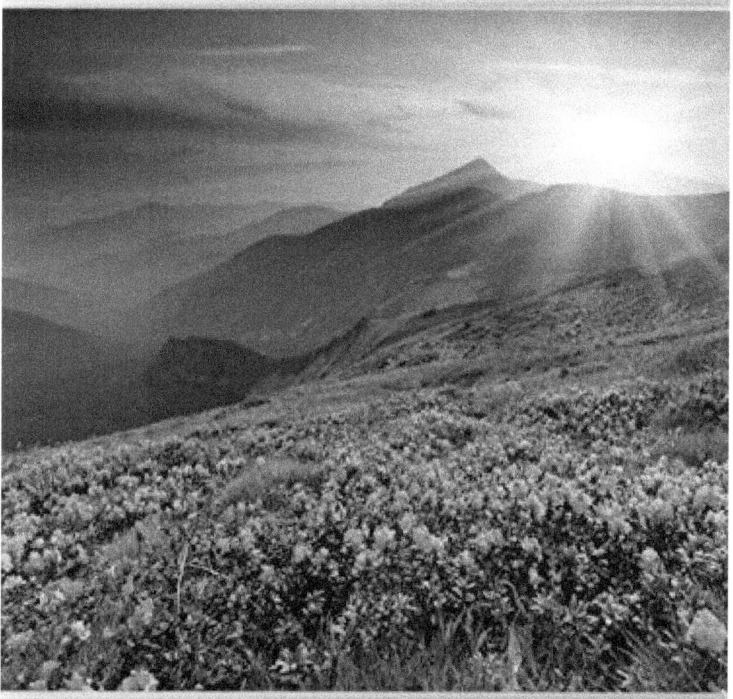

LANDSCAPE PHOTOGRAPHY
Photo Projects

How To Take Great
Landscape Photos

Steve Pease

There is a difference between someone who takes
pictures, and someone who makes pictures. Making
pictures is all about how you see the parts of the photos
you are creating. Practicing the art of taking great pictures
is the way to get them to be great. Do you want to learn to

make great photos? To be a success you need to practice.

This book contains projects for you to do that will help you focus on seeing things the way you need to see them to take great pictures instead of good pictures. Digital photography has become a part of almost every person's lives, we take pictures all the time, and of everything. We post them on websites and Facebook and send the shots from person to person through text messages. Picture taking has become billions of snapshots. The art of photography is being lost.

Learn to take great portraits

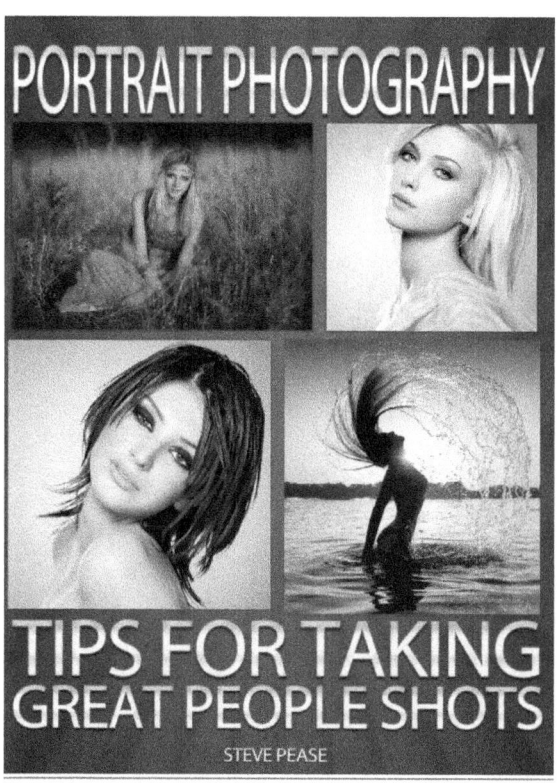

Why you should read this book.

I wrote this book to help solve this problem. I see hundreds of pictures that people take, and they want them to be great. They do not know the things they should look at and keep track of before they shoot the picture. If you read through this book, a few times and follow these tips, I promise your pictures will be much better. Even if you only use a couple tips, your pictures will be much better.

The book contains general tips that cover things you can do to improve portrait shots for any photos. Then there are tips that pertain to specific types of portrait shoots. Men, women, kids, groups, couples, and pets.

www.ingramcontent.com/pod-product-compliance
Lightning Source LLC
Chambersburg PA
CBHW051547170526
45165CB00002B/913